Our
PRESIDENTS

— THEIR LIVES AND STORIES —

ISBN-13: 978-0-8249-5916-6

Printed and bound in the U.S.A.

Published by Ideals Publications
A Guideposts Company
Nashville, Tennessee
www.idealsbooks.com

Library of Congress CIP data on file

10 9 8 7 6 5 4 3 2 1

Our
PRESIDENTS

— THEIR LIVES AND STORIES —

By Nancy J. Skarmeas

I do solemnly swear (or affirm) that I will faithfully execute the Office of the President of the United States, and will to the best of my ability, preserve, protect, and defend the Constitution of the United States.

IDEALS PUBLICATIONS

NASHVILLE, TENNESSEE

GEORGE WASHINGTON
1732–1799
FIRST PRESIDENT 1789–1797

A dignified, private man, George Washington won the office of president and the role of "Father of Our Country" due largely to his courageous and skillful leadership during the American Revolution. It was Washington who led the colonists in their revolt against the British: it was he who silently stole across the Delaware River to surprise and defeat the British at Princeton and Trenton, he who suffered with his men through the bleak winter of 1777–78 at Valley Forge, and he who, at Yorktown, proudly accepted the surrender of General Cornwallis that formally ended the Revolution. Thus it was General George Washington of Virginia whom the citizens of the new United States of America elected to lead them in their first bold steps as a nation.

Washington served carefully and well for two terms, aware that his every move decided the present fate of the nation and set a precedent for leaders to follow. Among his many accomplishments, Washington negotiated treaties with Spain and Great Britain, diffused the Whiskey Rebellion—the first challenge to federal authority in the new nation—and defined the process for choosing Supreme Court justices.

Little is known about the childhood and youth of our first president. Born in Westmoreland County, Virginia, in 1732, Washington was fatherless from an early age and raised mostly by his mother, Mary Ball Washington, and his half-brother Lawrence, from whom he inherited his Mount Vernon estate. The legend of the cherry tree and Washington's inability to lie were the invention of a biographer anxious to cash in on the great popularity of his subject. Washington married Martha Dandridge Custis in 1759. Although they had no children together, Washington adopted her two children from her first marriage. Before his presidency, in addition to his military career, Washington served in the Virginia House of Burgesses and as a delegate to the Continental Congress. He was the unanimous selection of his fellow delegates to be president of the Constitutional Convention; and he played a central role in the creation of the document on which our democracy was founded.

After two terms as president, George Washington retired from public life despite urgings from the public that he seek a third term. In his farewell address, he urged Americans to guard against division amongst themselves, to hold onto their faith, and to be wary of foreign involvements—advice which remains sound to this day. Washington retired to his beloved estate, Mount Vernon, where he died two years later in 1799.

The Continental Army set up winter camp at Valley Forge, Pennsylvania, in 1777 with their spirits sagging and their confidence shaken. A series of defeats at the hands of better-trained British forces had left the colonists wondering about their attempts at revolution. The winter took a heavy toll, and many died of cold and starvation; but by spring the Army was full of optimism and ready to take up its cause again, thanks to the leadership of General George Washington, who kept his men focused and their morale up. American artist Hy Hintermeister's painting Washington Observes Von Steuben Drilling the Troops at Valley Forge *commemorates Washington's heroism.*

George Washington was a large, muscular man whose hair, dark brown in youth, was powdered gray for formal occasions. Contrary to legend, Washington did not wear wooden dentures but had artificial teeth made from lead, ivory, and animal bone. This portrait by American artist Gilbert Stuart, one of many he painted of Washington, shows our first president in advanced age, with powder no longer necessary for his distinctive white hair.

To the efficacy and permanency of your union a government for the whole is indispensible. No alliances, however strict, among the parts can be an adequate substitute. They must inevitably experience the infractions and interruptions which all alliances in all times have experienced. Sensible of this momentous truth, you have improved upon your first essay by the adoption of a Constitution of government better calculated than your former for an intimate union and for the efficacious management of your common concerns. This government, the offspring of your own choice, uninfluenced and unawed, adopted upon full investigation and mature deliberation, completely free in its principles, in the distribution of its powers, uniting security with energy, and containing within itself a provision for its own amendment, has a just claim to your confidence and support. Respect for its authority, compliance with its laws, acquiescence in its measures, are duties enjoined by the fundamental maxims of true liberty. The basis of our political system is the right of the people to make and alter their constitutions of government. But the constitution which at any time exists till changed by an explicit and authentic act of the whole people is sacredly obligatory upon all. The very idea of the power and right of the people to establish government presupposes the duty of every individual to obey the established government. . . .

from George Washington's Farewell Address, delivered to his Cabinet on September 17, 1796, near the end of his second term in office

JOHN ADAMS
1735–1826
SECOND PRESIDENT 1797–1801

John Adams made a name for himself early in his career by defending the British soldiers accused of killing three colonists in the Boston Massacre. In a wave of anti-British hysteria, Adams remained resolute; believing that the soldiers had been provoked, he defended their innocence despite his strong colonial sympathies.

The Boston Massacre trial made Adams's name and character known throughout the colonies. A stubborn, principled man, Adams was also extremely intelligent and a brilliant lawyer. Born in 1735 in Braintree, Massachusetts, Adams was the descendant of Puritans and cousin to Samuel Adams, a signer of the Declaration of Independence. As a child, Adams dreamed of becoming a farmer; but his family sent him to Harvard, where he discovered his special calling for the practice of law. From a successful law practice in Boston, Adams went on to serve in the Massachusetts Legislature, the Continental Congress, and as vice president under George Washington. In 1797 he won the presidency in a closely contested election against Thomas Jefferson.

Adams's time in the White House was not peaceful. In what became known as the XYZ Affair, Adams refused to declare war against France after the French enraged Americans by demanding a large cash tribute before they would begin diplomatic negotiations. Cries of "millions for defense, but not a cent for tribute" were heard across America; but President Adams, realizing that his country was ill-prepared for war, patiently held his ground and averted all-out conflict. Peace secured, Adams faced the disapproval of many at home who believed he had failed to defend the nation's honor. Sensing his fading popularity, Adams supported the Alien and Sedition Acts, which he believed were a means of controlling opposition but which the public saw as an affront to their civil rights. Adams never regained popular support, and he left office after one term, bitter and disappointed.

John Adams is perhaps remembered best as the husband of Abigail Adams, who is considered by many to be the first American feminist. Abigail was an intelligent, highly educated, and opinionated individual who constantly reminded her husband to acknowledge the power of the nation's women. John and Abigail had five children and carried on a spirited and voluminous correspondence which has provided historians with a fascinating glimpse into the political, social, and personal lives of colonial Americans.

Upon leaving the White House, Adams returned to Massachusetts. He lived to see his son, John Quincy Adams, elected president in 1825 and died the following year on the Fourth of July, at the age of ninety.

Let us dare to read, think, speak, and write. Let every order and degree among the people rouse their attention and animate their resolution. Let them all become attentive to the grounds and principles of government, ecclesiastical and civil. Let us study the law of nature; search into the spirit of the British Constitution; read the histories of ancient ages; contemplate the great example of Greece and Rome; set before us the conduct of our own British ancestors, who have defined for us the inherent rights of mankind against foreign and domestic tyrants and usurpers, against arbitrary kings and cruel priests; in short, against the gates of earth and hell. Let us read and recollect and impress upon our souls the views and ends of our more immediate forefathers in exchanging their native country for a dreary, inhospitable wilderness. Let us examine into the nature of that power, and the cruelty of that oppression, which drove them from their homes. Recollect their amazing fortitude, their bitter sufferings—the hunger, the nakedness, the cold, which they patiently endured—the severe labors of clearing the grounds, building their houses, raising their provisions,

amidst dangers from wild beasts and savage men, before they had time or money or materials for commerce. Recollect the civil and religious principles and hopes and expectations which constantly supported and carried them through all hardships with patience and resignation. Let us recollect it was liberty, the hope of liberty for themselves and us and ours, which conquered all the discouragements, dangers, and trials. . . . Let the pulpit resound with the doctrines and sentiments of religious liberty. Let us hear the danger of thraldom to our consciences from ignorance, extreme poverty, and dependence; in short, from civil and political slavery. Let us see delineated before us the true map of man. Let us hear the dignity of his nature, and the noble rank he holds among the works of God—that consenting to slavery is a sacrilegious breach of trust, as offensive in the sight of God as it is derogatory from our own honor or interest or happiness—and that God Almighty has promulgated from heaven liberty, peace, and goodwill to man!

from John Adams's article in the Boston Gazette in 1765, written in response to the Stamp Act imposed on the colonies by Great Britain

John Adams was a short, stocky man who, despite poor health all of his life, lived to the age of ninety, exceptionally long for his era. The portrait at the right is the work of American artist Gilbert Stuart, who came of age during the Revolution and painted most of the great leaders of the day.

THOMAS JEFFERSON
1743–1826
THIRD PRESIDENT 1801–1809

Our third president, Thomas Jefferson, was born in 1743 at Shadwell Plantation in Virginia. All of his life, he was a man of great intellect and insatiable curiosity. His interests outside of politics and government included such diverse fields as architecture, botany, animal husbandry, and meteorology. Jefferson designed his home—the elegant Monticello; he founded the University of Virginia; and he improved his own daily life with such inventions as the swivel chair, the adjustable drafting table, and an instrument that allowed him to make simultaneous copies of his letters and documents.

Of course, Jefferson also wrote the Declaration of Independence, served as governor of Virginia, minister to France, secretary of state, and, for eight years, president of the United States. During his two terms in the White House, Jefferson was an outspoken proponent of states' rights, opposing any measures that he felt were instruments of a too-powerful federal government. Jefferson also took the first small step toward the abolition of slavery when he outlawed the importation of slaves to the United States. Another of his administration's great contributions to American history was the opening and exploration of the West. For fifteen million dollars—what amounted to three cents an acre—Jefferson purchased the Louisiana Territory from France. The Louisiana Purchase doubled the size of the United States, adding all or part of fifteen present-day states. As a follow-up to the purchase, Jefferson commissioned Meriwether Lewis and William Clark to lead an expedition across the Continental Divide to the Pacific, beginning the great western expansion of America.

Thomas Jefferson was one of our greatest presidents and our greatest citizens. He was a man of intelligence and integrity, a man who, as much as he believed in the government he helped create, equally believed that government was invalid unless it respected the rights of every individual it governed.

Thomas Jefferson married Martha Wayles Skelton when he was twenty-eight years old. Together they had two daughters and ten years of happy marriage. When she died in 1782, Jefferson turned all his energies to public life. After leaving the presidency, Jefferson returned to Monticello. He died there on July 4th, 1826, only hours before the death of John Adams, on the fiftieth anniversary of the signing of the Declaration of Independence.

Thomas Jefferson's passion for architecture found expression in his stately Virginia home, Monticello. The home and its surrounding landscape were entirely Jefferson's design. Among the estate's innovative and original features were a clock which showed one face on the inside of the house and another on the outside, a shaft lined with stone to ventilate his outhouse, and a dumbwaiter to deliver goods from his cellar to his dining room. Today, Monticello and its surrounding gardens are maintained as a memorial to the former president.

All, too, will bear in mind this sacred principle, that though the will of the majority is in all cases to prevail, that will to be rightful must be reasonable; that the minority possesses their equal rights, which equal law must protect, and to violate would be oppression. Let us then, fellow citizens, unite with one heart and one mind. Let us restore to social intercourse that harmony and affliction without which liberty and even life itself are but dreary things. And let us reflect that, having banished from our land that religious intolerance under which mankind so long bled and suffered, we have yet gained little if we countenance a political intolerance as despotic, as wicked, and capable of as bitter and bloody persecutions. . . . every difference of opinion is not a difference of principle. We have called by different names brethren of the same principle. We are all Republicans. We are all Federalists. If there be any among us who wish to dissolve this Union or change its republican form, let them stand undisturbed as monuments of the safety with which error of opinion may be tolerated where reason is left free to combat it. I know, indeed, that some honest men fear that a Republican government can not be strong, that this government is not strong enough; but would the honest patriot, in the full tide of successful experiment, abandon a government which has so far kept us free and firm on the theoretic and visionary fear that this Government, the world's best hope, may by possibility, want energy to preserve itself? I trust not. I believe this, on contrary, the strongest government on earth. I believe it is the only one where every man, at the call of the law, would fly to the standard of the law, and would meet invasions of the public order as his personal concern. Sometimes it is said that man cannot be trusted with the government of himself. Can he, then, be trusted with the government of others? Or have we found angels in the form of kings to govern for him? Let history answer this question.

from Thomas Jefferson's first Inaugural Address, delivered in Washington, D.C., on March 4, 1801

JAMES MADISON
1751–1836
FOURTH PRESIDENT 1809–1817

Ashort, slightly built man, who, plagued all his life by shyness, spoke in a soft, unassuming voice, James Madison played a powerful role in the establishment and enforcement of American independence. Along with his wife, Dolley, who herself earned fame for her heroism during the British siege of Washington during the War of 1812, Madison spent eight years in the White House at a very critical time in American history.

Born in Virginia, Madison grew up at Montpelier, his family's plantation near the Blue Ridge Mountains. He was educated at the College of New Jersey (now known as Princeton) and graduated with the intention of becoming a lawyer but instead got caught up in the revolutionary spirit sweeping the colonies. Known as the "Father of the Constitution," Madison was a leader at the Constitutional Convention of 1787, drafting much of the document, including the Bill of Rights. Madison went on from the Convention to a successful career in public service. He represented Virginia in the House of Representatives and served for eight years as secretary of state. In 1808 Madison, the Jeffersonian Republican candidate for president, soundly defeated his Federalist opponent in the national election. He served two terms in the White House, with the bulk of his energies consumed by the conflict with Great Britain that culminated in the War of 1812.

At the center of that conflict was the British navy's refusal to respect the rights of American ships at sea. For years British ships had been impressing American sailors and seizing American goods. In 1812 President Madison, convinced that Britain would not respond to peaceful means, asked Congress to declare war. The war lasted two years and ended with the main issues unresolved. Nonetheless, domestic industry had flourished in the void created by embargoes on British goods; no longer were Americans dependent upon foreign imports for survival. Under the leadership of James Madison, who would not let American rights be disregarded, a new American independence was assured.

At the completion of his second term, James and Dolley Madison left the White House for Montpelier. There, he concentrated on running the plantation but also remained active in Virginia and national politics until his death in 1836.

Dolley Madison was one of the most popular first ladies ever to live at the White House. She was known for her vivacious personality, her active social calendar, and, after the War of 1812, her heroism. In August of 1814, with the British advancing on Washington and the president out of town, Mrs. Madison remained at the White House, determined to save the house, or at least its valuables, from destruction. She wrote to her sister: "I am still here within sound of the canon! Mr. Madison comes not; may God protect him. . . . I insist on waiting until the large picture of George Washington is secured, and it requires to be unscrewed from the wall." Mrs. Madison saved the Gilbert Stuart portrait of Washington, as well as many other White House treasures, before finally agreeing to flee the capitol. The White House and much of the city were soon thereafter burned by the British.

James Madison stood just five-feet, four-inches and weighed no more than one hundred pounds. The smallest of our presidents, he was meticulous about his appearance and dressed almost always in black. In contrast to his wife, the vivacious Dolley Madison, James Madison was a quiet, reserved man. This portrait was painted by American artist Chester Harding.

The present situation of the world is indeed without parallel, and that of our own country is full of difficulties. The pressure of these, too, is the more severely felt because they have fallen upon us at a moment when the national prosperity being at a height not before attained, the contrast resulting from the change has been rendered the more striking. Under the benign influence of our republican institutions, and the maintenance of peace with all nations whilst so many of them were engaged in bloody and wasteful wars, the fruits of a just policy were enjoyed in an unrivaled growth of our faculties and resources. . . . It is a precious reflection that the transition from this prosperous condition of our country to the scene which has for some time been distressing us is not chargeable on any unwarrantable views, nor, as I trust, on any involuntary errors in the public councils. Indulging no passions which trespass on the rights or repose of other nations, it has been the true glory of the United States to cultivate peace by observing justice, and to entitle themselves to the respect of the nations at war by fulfilling their neutral obligations with the most scrupulous impartiality. If there be candor in the world, the truth of these assertions will not be questions; posterity will at least do justice to them.

from James Madison's first Inaugural Address, delivered March 4, 1809

Never did a government commence under auspices so favorable, nor ever was success so complete. If we look to the history of other nations, ancient or modern, we find no example of a growth so rapid, so gigantic, of a people so prosperous and happy. In contemplating what we have still to perform, the heart of every citizen must expand with joy when he reflects how near our government has approached to perfection; that in respect to it we have no essential improvement to make; that the great object is to preserve in it the essential principles and features which characterize it, and that that is to be done by preserving the virtue and enlightening the minds of the people; and as a security against foreign dangers to adopt such arrangements as are indispensible to the support of our independence, our rights and liberties. If we persevere in the career in which we have advanced so far and in the path already traced, we can not fail, under the favor of a gracious Providence, to attain the high destiny which seems to await us.

from James Monroe's first Inaugural Address, delivered in Washington, D.C., March 4, 1817

James Monroe was a good-hearted man who was liked and respected by all who knew him. Thomas Jefferson, the former president under whom Monroe had served as minister to Great Britain, once said of the fifth president, "Turn his soul wrong side outward and there is not a speck on it." During the Revolution, Monroe rose from lieutenant to major. He was present at George Washington's historic crossing of the Delaware River prior to the Battle of Trenton in December of 1776, and he survived the winter of 1777–78 at Valley Forge, Pennsylvania. This painting of Monroe is the work of American artist Samuel F. B. Morse.

JAMES MONROE
1758–1831
FIFTH PRESIDENT 1817–1825

stand, was protected by the Constitution, and that the nation could survive part slave and part free. Monroe supported the Missouri Compromise of 1821, which drew a line at latitude 36°30' dividing the free North from the slaveholding South. According to the Compromise, Missouri was admitted to the Union as a slave state, Maine as a free state, and the delicate balance between slave and free states was preserved. Days to come, however, would prove the Missouri Compromise inadequate and the division it formalized incompatible with the survival of the Union. President Monroe made a more lasting contribution to American history with the Monroe Doctrine, which warned the nations of Europe that the Americas were no longer open to colonization or exploitation. This strong statement entered the United States into world politics and remains at the foundation of American foreign policy more than two hundred years later.

As a student at the College of William and Mary in Williamsburg, Virginia, young James Monroe quit his studies to join the Continental army; his commitment to his country would never waver. Before his election as president, Monroe served as a member of the Continental Congress, a United States senator, minister to France, governor of Virginia, minister to Great Britain, and secretary of state. After a lifetime of public service, he retired to Virginia with Elizabeth, who had lived a quiet, private life as first lady. After his wife's death, the former president moved to New York City, where he lived with his daughter and her family until his death in 1831. Monroe was the third of our first five presidents to die on Independence Day.

James Monroe took office at a rather peaceful time in American history. The battle for independence was won, and the tragically divisive issue of slavery had yet to reach a crisis point. The Monroe administration was popularly known as the "Era of Good Feeling," as Monroe—the warm, generous, good-hearted son of a Virginia planter—and the Jeffersonian Republican party enjoyed the almost unanimous support of the entire nation. A veteran of the American Revolution and a lifelong public servant, Monroe easily won two consecutive terms as president. He and his wife, Elizabeth Kortright Monroe, had two daughters, one of whom was married in the first wedding ever held at the White House.

Although "good feeling" ruled the day during the Monroe years, the question of slavery still demanded some attention. Like so many of his contemporaries, Monroe believed that slavery, whatever one's moral

JOHN QUINCY ADAMS
1767–1848
SIXTH PRESIDENT 1825–1829

A brilliant man with a flair for negotiation, John Quincy Adams, the son of second president John Adams, experienced firsthand the momentous action of the American fight for independence and the founding of the nation. As a boy, Adams traveled extensively, received education from the most respected tutors, and lived a comfortable life of great privilege.

As was family tradition, Adams attended Harvard University. Not long after his graduation, his family connections–and his fluency in Dutch–won him appointment by George Washington as minister to the Netherlands. During his father's administration, young Adams served as minister to Prussia. On his return to the United States, Adams won his first elective office, a seat in the Massachusetts State Senate. This led to a seat in the U.S. Senate and, in 1814, appointment to a special delegation sent to negotiate the Treaty of Ghent, which formally ended the War of 1812. Adams ran for president in 1824 and was elected in a tight four-way race courtesy of his strong support in his native New England.

Adams's single term in the White House was largely uneventful. His greatest achievement was a comprehensive program of internal improvements. Adams was the first president to believe that the Constitution gave the federal government authority and responsibility to build roads and canals, and he did much to extend and modernize both. Adams left his boldest mark on history, however, after his days in the White House when, as a Representative from Massachusetts, he fought courageously against slavery at a time when most public figures were unwilling to do so.

John Quincy Adams died in 1848 in the U.S. Capitol building after suffering a stroke on the floor of the House. He was survived by his wife, Louisa, and one of their three sons. Adams's passing was observed by fellow Massachusetts citizen Theodore Parker, who recognized the former president's achievement: "The slave has lost a champion who gained new ardor and new strength the longer he fought; America has lost a man who loved her with his heart; religion has lost a supporter; freedom an unfailing friend; and mankind a noble vindicator of our inalienable rights."

John Quincy Adams proved his skills as a statesman while serving as secretary of state under James Monroe. He drafted the Monroe Doctrine, the bold foreign policy statement which declared the Americas off limits to European colonization; he negotiated with Great Britain to determine the American border with Canada; and he helped the U. S. add Florida to its territories. Adams, considered only an average president, is remembered as one of the greatest to ever fill the position of secretary of state.

George Washington once remarked of a young John Quincy Adams, "Mr. Adams is the most valuable public character we have abroad. . . . there remains no doubt in my mind that he will prove himself to be the ablest of all our diplomatic corps." Washington's prediction proved correct as Adams spent almost fifteen years serving American interests abroad before he became president. This portrait of Adams is the work of American painter George P. A. Healy.

Ten years of peace, at home and abroad, have assuaged the animosities of political contention and blended into harmony the most discordant elements of public opinion. There still remains one effort of magnanimity, one sacrifice of prejudice and passion, to be made by the individuals throughout the nation who have heretofore followed the standards of political party. It is that of discarding every element of rancor against each other, of embracing as countrymen and friends, and of yielding to talents and virtue alone that confidence which in times of contention for principle was bestowed only upon those who bore the badge of party communion.

from John Quincy Adams's Inaugural Address, delivered March 4, 1825

ANDREW JACKSON
1767–1845
SEVENTH PRESIDENT 1829–1837

Charismatic and combative, Andrew Jackson met the challenge of the presidency as he did everything else in life—head on. In the course of two terms, the power of his will and of his belief in the necessity of a strong, unyielding federal government substantially redefined the office of president.

Jackson's birthplace remains the subject of dispute. Both Union County, North Carolina, and neighboring Lancaster County in South Carolina claim him as a native, and no records exist to prove either state wrong. Jackson's father died before he was born, and his mother when he was only fourteen. As a boy, Jackson received a good education; legend has it that when the Declaration of Independence was signed, nine-year-old Andrew read it aloud from the newspapers to illiterate family members and neighbors. Jackson joined the colonial army when he was just thirteen and later fought in the War of 1812 and the First Seminole War. His toughness and heroism in battle earned him the nickname "Old Hickory." Before his election to the presidency in 1828, Jackson served as a United States representative and a senator for his adopted home state of Tennessee.

As president, Jackson stood firmly on the side of a strong central government at a time when the majority of his fellow southerners were fighting hard for states' rights, with the issue of slavery at the heart of the battle. Jackson used his presidential veto liberally to oppose Congress and all else who did not share his vision. The most controversial of his vetoes was on the re-charter of the Second Bank of the United States. Jackson wanted the bank shut down because it persisted in printing paper money without gold or silver to back it up. His will prevailed despite the strong disapproval of the Congress.

Tall and lean, with thick red hair turned gray and a gaunt, striking face, Andrew Jackson had a physical presence to match his temperament. Most of his public life was marked by controversy. His wife, Rachel Donelson Jackson, was still legally married to her first husband when she wed Jackson; and despite the fact that the legal technicalities of the situation were eventually

resolved, Mrs. Jackson remained the object of much criticism. Jackson valiantly defended his wife's honor; and in 1806 he challenged one of her critics, Charles Dickinson, to a duel, which ended with Dickinson dead and Jackson badly wounded. Despite the controversy, and despite the fact that Jackson angered as many as he inspired, he was a strong and effective president whose confident use of the authority of his office set a precedent for every president to come.

When he left office, Andrew Jackson returned to the Hermitage, his plantation in Nashville. Rachel Jackson had died in 1828, only months before her husband's inauguration as president. Jackson spent his retirement alone and died in Nashville in 1845.

Andrew Jackson led American forces to their greatest victory in the War of 1812 on January 8, 1815, two full weeks after the war was officially ended. The Battle of New Orleans, in which Jackson led a small group of Americans in their defense of the city against a much larger, better trained British contingent, made "Old Hickory" a national hero and paved his way to the presidency. Only after the battle was completed did the news reach New Orleans that the Treaty of Ghent had been signed –in December of 1814–and peace formally secured.

The time at which I stand before you is full of interest. The eyes of all nations are fixed on our Republic. The event of the existing crisis will be decisive in the opinion of mankind of the practicability of our federal system of government. Great is the stake placed in our hands; great is the responsibility which must rest upon the people of the United States. Let us realize the importance of the attitude in which we stand before the world. Let us exercise forbearance and firmness. Let us extricate our country from the dangers which surround it and learn wisdom from the lessons they inculcate.

Deeply impressed with the truth of these observations, and under the obligation of that solemn oath I am about to take, I shall continue to exert all my faculties to maintain the just powers of the Constitution and to transmit unimpaired to posterity the blessings of our Federal Union. . . . Constantly bearing in mind that in entering into society "individuals must give up a share of liberty to preserve the rest," it will be my desire so to discharge my duties as to foster with our brethren in all parts of the country a spirit of liberal concession and compromise, and by reconciling our fellow citizens to those partial sacrifices which they must unavoidably make for the preservation of the greater good, to recommend our invaluable Government and Union to the confidences and affections of the American people.

from Andrew Jackson's second Inaugural Address, delivered March 4, 1833

MARTIN VAN BUREN
1782–1862
EIGHTH PRESIDENT 1837–1841

Born in 1782, Martin Van Buren grew up in poverty in Kinderhook, New York, in a family where the Dutch language was spoken and Dutch customs observed. As a young man, Van Buren married his childhood sweetheart, Hannah Hoes, with whom he had four sons. He was an optimistic man who enjoyed public life. Before his election as president in 1836, he served as a senator from New York, governor of New York, secretary of state, and vice president.

Van Buren came to office as president just months after the Panic of 1837, in which the nation's banks refused to convert paper money to silver and gold and thereby created a major depression. The depression lasted until 1843, two years after Van Buren left office, and marred all of Van Buren's short term as president. Nonetheless, Van Buren's administration was not without its successes. A cautious and principled man, Van Buren avoided war with Great Britain in a dispute over the border between Maine and Canada by beginning negotiations that led eventually to the Webster-Ashburton Treaty, which determined the present-day border. He established the independent treasury system, which required that money owed to the United States be paid in gold or silver rather than paper. Van Buren opposed the annexation of Texas, which he feared would upset the balance between free and slave states and lead the nation closer to civil war.

In retirement, Van Buren came to believe that the complete abolition of slavery was the only answer to the division troubling the Union. In 1848, with the son of John Quincy Adams as his running mate, Van Buren ran again for the presidency, this time as the candidate of the Free Soil Party. The Van Buren-Adams ticket received enough votes to affect the outcome of the election, but its abolitionist message went largely unheeded. Following his defeat, Van Buren retired for good from public life and lived his remaining years on his farm in his hometown of Kinderhook. He died there in 1862 with the country in the midst of the Civil War.

This provident forecast has been verified by time. Half a century, teeming with extraordinary events, and elsewhere producing astonishing results, has passed along; but on our institutions it has left no injurious mark. From a small community we have risen to a people powerful in numbers and in strength; but with our increase has gone hand in hand the progress of just principles. The privileges, civil and religious, of the humblest individual are still sacredly protected at home, and while the valor and fortitude of our people have removed far from us the slightest apprehension of foreign power, they have not yet induced us in a single instance to forget what is right. . . . We have learned by experience a fruitful lesson—that an implicit and undeviating adherence to the principles on which we set out can carry us prosperously onward through all the conflicts of circumstance and vicissitudes inseparable from the lapse of years.

The success that has thus attended our great experiment is in itself sufficient cause for gratitude, on account of the happiness it has actually conferred and the example it has unanswerably given. But to me, my fellow citizens, looking forward to the far distant future with ardent prayers and confiding hopes, this retrospect presents a ground for still deeper delight. It impresses upon my mind a firm belief that the perpetuity of our institutions depends on ourselves; that if we maintain the principles on which they were established they are destined to confer their benefits upon countless generations yet to come, and that America will present to every friend of mankind the cheering proof that a popular government wisely formed, is wanting in no element of endurance or strength.

from Martin Van Buren's Inaugural Address,
delivered March 4, 1837

Known as "The Red Fox of Kinderhook" and "The Little Magician," Martin Van Buren was a skilled politician who knew just what to say and when to say it. He was a small man who paid careful attention to his dress, a habit which, combined with his reputation as a sly politician, led many to see him as pompous and phony. Those who knew Van Buren personally, however, knew him as an honest, generous man. Van Buren's refined manners and fastidious habits were the target of William Henry Harrison's campaign against him in 1840. Harrison and his supporters portrayed Van Buren as a weak and ineffectual leader, a great contrast to the rugged man of the frontier they boasted their candidate to be.

WILLIAM HENRY HARRISON
1773–1841
NINTH PRESIDENT 1841

It is union that we want, not of a party for the sake of that party, but a union of the whole country for the sake of the whole country, for the defense of its interests and its honor against foreign aggression, for the defense of those principles for which our ancestors so gloriously contended.

from William Henry Harrison's Inaugural Address, delivered March 4, 1841

William Henry Harrison's 1840 presidential campaign was dubbed "The Log Cabin Campaign" by supporters who hoped to portray their candidate as a true man of the people, in contrast to opponent Martin Van Buren, who was an easterner with refined manners and appearance. While Harrison had spent much of his adult life on the western frontier, he was a Virginian by birth and a man of great wealth. Nonetheless, the American people embraced Harrison's rugged frontier image, thanks in great part to legends of his heroism in the Indian Wars.

William Henry Harrison, the son of Benjamin Harrison, a signer of the Declaration of Independence, was born to wealth and privilege on Berkeley Plantation in Virginia. He was to achieve fame and success, however, as a rugged, plain-spoken man of the frontier.

As a child, Harrison had dreams of becoming a doctor; and after receiving basic education from tutors, he went on to college and medical school. At the age of eighteen, however, Harrison abandoned his education and joined the army to fight in the Indian Wars in the Northwest Territory. For most of the next fifty years, Harrison remained on the frontier as a professional soldier and a public official.

Harrison's road to the presidency began with an appointment as secretary of the Northwest Territory. Later, he was selected by the people to be the region's delegate to the United States House of Representatives. After another stint in the army during the War of 1812, Harrison again turned to public life, serving as a congressman for the state of Ohio before he made his run for the presidency in 1840. In a campaign of slogans and personalities, Harrison ran as the rugged man of the frontier. His campaign slogan, "Tippecanoe and Tyler, too," was a tribute to his heroism in the Battle of Tippecanoe back in the Indian Wars. Harrison won the presidency handily over Martin Van Buren, who was crippled by the depression that had engulfed his time in office.

At sixty-eight, Harrison was one of the oldest men ever elected to the presidency. He also would have the unfortunate distinction of serving the shortest term. During his inauguration ceremony, Harrison caught cold. Within a month, he was dead of pneumonia, leaving his vice president, John Tyler, to assume the office and duties of the president.

William Henry Harrison was the father of ten children, only four of whom lived long enough to see their father elected president. His wife, Anna Tuthill Symmes Harrison, never lived in the White House with her husband. She had been planning to travel to Washington from Ohio in the spring after his inauguration, but he died before she could make the trip.

JOHN TYLER
1790–1862
TENTH PRESIDENT 1841–1845

case of a president's death, but there were many who believed it did not call for the vice president to assume the office of the president. Mockingly called "His Accidency" by opponents, Tyler never received the complete support or respect of either his own cabinet or his own party. In 1841, after Tyler refused to sign legislation creating the Third Bank of the United States, all but one member of his cabinet resigned, further weakening his already tenuous hold on presidential authority. He left office after one term. Eventually, Tyler's assertion that the vice president in fact became president in the event of death or assassination would win favor; today it is considered constitutionally mandated.

John Tyler achieved another first in the White House. He was the first president to be married while in office. For Tyler it was a second marriage. His first wife, Letitia Christian, died during his administration. In 1844, only nine months after the death of his first wife, the president married Julia Gardiner in a New York City ceremony kept secret from the public and all but one of Tyler's own children. With his two wives, Tyler had fourteen children—seven of whom were born after his term as president—making him the most prolific American president. Tyler died in 1862 in Richmond, Virginia. He is remembered by historians not as a great president, but as a man whose experience was one more test of the young nation's constitutional foundation.

A graceful southern gentleman, John Tyler assumed the presidency upon the death of William Henry Harrison. Born at Greenway Plantation on Virginia's James River and educated at the College of William and Mary, Tyler, a former governor of Virginia and United States senator, was the first vice president to accede to the office after the death of a president, and he struggled for the remainder of his term against those who believed his authority to be less than complete.

The Constitution called for the vice president to assume the duties and powers of the president in the

I am determined to uphold the Constitution . . . to the utmost of my ability and in defiance of all personal consequences. What may happen to an individual is of little importance, but the Constitution of the country, or any of its great and clear principles and provisions, is too sacred to be surrendered under any circumstances whatever by those who are charged with its protection and defense.

John Tyler, 1842

JAMES K. POLK
1795–1849
ELEVENTH PRESIDENT 1845–1849

James Knox Polk is often called by historians the greatest one-term president. An ardent believer in Manifest Destiny—the popular expression for the belief that America was divinely intended to extend its borders from the Atlantic Ocean west to the Pacific—Polk achieved much in four years, most of it concerned with extending the territory of the United States. A middle-Tennessee native, Polk was a hardworking and ambitious man who won the approval of contemporaries and successors alike, among them thirty-third president Harry S Truman, who said of Polk: "A great president. Said what he intended to do and did it all." Before winning the presidency, Polk had served as Speaker of the House of Representatives and governor of Tennessee.

Manifest Destiny was the guiding principle of the Polk administration. His Democratic party's slogan of "Fifty-four forty or fight!" referred to the western land between 42° and 54°40' latitude, which Americans believed should be their own. For years Great Britain had made similar claims, and the two nations were deadlocked. Polk fought hard to win the land and, in the end, agreed to the Oregon Treaty which, whereas it fell short of the famous parameters, guaranteed to the United States the land that is now the states of Washington and Oregon. Polk also led the United States into the Mexican War, which settled the conflict over the Texas-Mexico border and resulted in land annexation in excess of 500,000 square miles, the largest addition to the Union since the Louisiana Purchase.

James Polk did not seek election to a second term. After the inauguration of his successor, he and his wife, Sarah, embarked upon a tour of the southeastern United States, making their way toward Nashville, where they intended to spend their retirement in a newly purchased home they called Polk Place. The former president was weak from cholera by the time he arrived in Nashville, however, and within three weeks he was dead at the young age of fifty-four.

Samuel and Jane Polk took their infant son, James, to the local Presbyterian church for baptism but left before the ceremony was completed due to an argument with the minister. Nonetheless, James Polk, the future president, was raised as a Presbyterian and attended services regularly until the age of thirty-eight when, at a camp meeting, he was inspired to convert to Methodism. It was not until shortly before his death, however, that Polk finally was baptized a Methodist.

James and Sarah Polk's White House was a distinctively different place than it had been in previous administrations. Sarah Childress Polk made some immediate changes upon arrival in Washington in 1845. Mrs. Polk banned wine, dancing, and card playing in the president's house and cut down on formal entertaining, although she was said to have enjoyed her duties as official Washington hostess. Mrs. Polk, like her husband, believed in hard work above all else, and the White House they occupied was a quiet, business-like place. During the second year of James Polk's presidency, Sarah Polk became his personal secretary in hopes of lightening the immense work load he had undertaken. The president regularly sought input from his wife on the issues before him, and together they were a productive and efficient team. The Polks, married twenty-five years, had no children.

Who shall assign limits to the achievements of free minds and free hands under the protection of this glorious Union? No treason to mankind since the organization of society would be equal in atrocity to that of him who would lift his hand to destroy it. He would overthrow the noblest structure of human wisdom, which protects himself and his fellow man. He would stop the progress of free government and involve his country either in anarchy or despotism. He would extinguish the fire of liberty, which warms and animates the hearts of happy millions and invites all the nations of the earth to imitate our example. If he say that error and wrong are committed in the administration of the Government, let him remember that nothing human can be perfect, and that under no other system of government revealed by Heaven or devised by man has reason been allowed so free and so broad a scope to combat error. Has the sword of despots proven to be a safer or surer instrument of reform in government than enlightened reason? Does he expect to find among the ruins of this Union a happier abode for our swarming millions than they now have under it? Every lover of this country must shudder at the thought of the possibility of its dissolution, and will be ready to adopt the patriotic sentiment, "Our Federal Union, it must be preserved."

from James Polk's Inaugural Address, delivered March 4, 1845

ZACHARY TAYLOR
1784–1850
TWELFTH PRESIDENT 1849–1850

For more than half a century, during which kingdoms and empires have fallen, this Union has stood unshaken. The patriots who formed it have long since descended to the grave; yet still it remains, the proudest monument to their memory. In my judgement, its dissolution would be the greatest of calamities. . . . Upon its preservation must depend our own happiness and that of countless generations to come. Whatever dangers may threaten it, I shall stand by it and maintain it in its integrity to the full extent of the obligations imposed and the power conferred upon me by the Constitution.

Zachary Taylor, speaking in 1848, the year he was elected president

Known as "Old Rough and Ready" for his toughness and heroism during the Mexican War, Zachary Taylor was a good-hearted, unpretentious man who, due to a lifelong battle with a stutter, spoke in a slow, studied manner. A direct descendant of *Mayflower* Pilgrim William Brewster, Taylor grew up on his father's plantation in Kentucky, on the western edge of the American frontier.

Never a politician, Taylor considered the military his career. He fought in the War of 1812, the Black Hawk War, the Second Seminole War, and the Mexican War, all the while moving his wife Peggy and their four children with him from fort to fort across the southeastern United States. It was in 1847, in the Battle of Buena Vista during the Mexican War, that Taylor rose to the level of general and became a national hero. In a fierce battle, Taylor narrowly escaped serious injury on two occasions while courageously leading his men to the defeat of a much larger Mexican army.

Returning from war a hero, Taylor easily won the Whig nomination for president in 1848. In the national election, Old Rough and Ready, who himself had never voted in a presidential election and never run for public office, won a close three-way race, defeating Democrat Lewis Cass and former president Martin Van Buren, who represented the Free Soil Party.

Taylor's time in office was consumed mostly by the issue of slavery. Taylor, who was a slaveholder himself, opposed the expansion of slavery into the territories and new states but believed that preservation of the Union must be the ultimate goal of all Americans. He vowed to veto the Compromise of 1850, which he believed made too many concessions to southern slave states. This stand won him widespread disapproval in the South, where it was seen as a federal intrusion into their rights, and among moderates, who believed that compromise was the only hope for the Union.

Zachary Taylor served sixteen months as president. He died in office in July of 1850 of what the doctors called *cholera morbus,* a gastro-intestinal illness contracted after a meal of cherries and iced milk. Sanitation was poor in the hot, humid Washington summers, and Taylor's illness was not uncommon. Taylor's wife, Peggy, in poor health before her husband's death, lived only two more years. Three of their four children survived them.

Millard Fillmore, elected vice president in 1848, acceded to the presidency in the summer of 1850 upon the sudden death of President Zachary Taylor. Fillmore inherited the reins of a nation badly divided and on the verge of civil war. The highlight of his administration was the Compromise of 1850, a measure which Taylor had stubbornly opposed but which Fillmore believed was the best chance for securing peace between North and South.

Fillmore came to Washington, D.C., from New York's Finger Lakes region, where he was born in the first year of the nineteenth century in a log cabin on his parents' farm. As a child, Fillmore received no formal education. Not until the age of seventeen, when a library opened in the small town of New Hope where he was serving as an apprentice to a clothmaker, did he discover his love of books and learning. Two years later, Fillmore enrolled at a local school. His first teacher, Abigail Powers, would eventually become his wife. Together they had two children and amassed a personal library of over four thousand volumes. Mrs. Fillmore, as first lady, worked to create the first permanent library in the White House.

Fillmore brought the skills of a long career in law and public service to the White House and put them to work in his best efforts to preserve the Union. Like most leaders of his day, Fillmore believed that the United States could survive half slave and half free, and he believed that the rights of slaveholders were protected by the Constitution. The Compromise of 1850, which Fillmore supported wholeheartedly, admitted California to the Union as a free state and abolished the slave trade in Washington, D.C. But it was no abolitionist's bill. For the slave states the Compromise included the Fugitive Slave Law, which held northern states responsible for the return of escaped slaves found within their borders. At best, it was a temporary solution to the nation's problems, forestalling but not preventing civil war.

Support of the Compromise of 1850 cost Fillmore the chance at a second term, as northern members of his Whig party could not forgive him for supporting the Fugitive Slave Law. After one term, Fillmore retired from public life. Within sixteen months, personal tragedy struck twice: Abigail Fillmore died of pneumonia after catching cold at the Pierce inauguration; and one year later, the Fillmores' daughter, Mary, died suddenly of cholera. In his grief, the former president embarked on an extended trip across the U.S. and Europe, settling finally near his childhood home in Buffalo, New York. In 1856 Fillmore accepted the nomination of the American, or Know-Nothing Party—a group seeking to create stricter immigration laws—and ran again for the presidency, winning twenty-one percent of the vote against James Buchanan. He died in 1874 in Buffalo.

FRANKLIN PIERCE
1804–1869
FOURTEENTH PRESIDENT 1853–1857

Franklin Pierce, the son of a Revolutionary War veteran, was born in a log cabin on the banks of the Contoocook River in Hillsborough County, New Hampshire. He proved himself a superior student in childhood and later at Bowdoin College in Maine, where among his closest friends was the aspiring young author Nathaniel Hawthorne. After college Pierce returned to New Hampshire to set up a law practice.

Pierce did not seek the presidency; rather it fell in his lap at a time when the nation's political parties were as divided as the people they served. After a career in the New Hampshire Legislature and the United States Congress, Pierce had returned again to his New Hampshire law practice, tired of the fast-paced life of Washington politics. But in 1852 his Democratic party could not agree upon a candidate and, late in the convention balloting, Pierce's name was put forth as a compromise candidate. To the surprise of many, it was accepted. That fall, Franklin Pierce won the national election and became the fourteenth president of the United States.

Pierce likely wished he had never left the quiet of New Hampshire. Only months before his inauguration, his young son was killed in a train accident, the third and last of the Pierces' children to die at an early age. He and his wife Jane went to the White House in the depths of depression. Their experience of the presidency did little to lift their spirits. Like his immediate predecessors, Pierce proved powerless in his attempts to stem the tide of civil war. The Kansas-Nebraska Act, to which he gave his full support, was aimed at easing the conflict in the midwestern territories by establishing popular sovereignty. The idea was to allow residents to choose for themselves whether their states would be slave or free. The results were disastrous, with Kansas erupting into a bitter, bloody conflict. What the nation needed was not popular sovereignty but strong decisive leadership. Franklin Pierce proved unequal to the task.

Pierce, a devout Christian who would not so much as open mail on Sundays, left the White House after one troubled term. He and Jane returned to New Hampshire, where they sought solace and relief from their grief for their three sons. In later years, Pierce openly opposed the Civil War, calling the bloodshed a tragedy and the goal of preserving the Union by force an impossibility. After the assassination of President Lincoln, an angry mob attacked Pierce's home, confusing his opposition to war with opposition to the Union. Pierce died in 1869 in Concord, New Hampshire, not far from the riverside log cabin where he was born.

Franklin Pierce is the only United States president to hail from New Hampshire. He was never happy with the fast-paced city life of Washington and, after his difficult years as president, returned gladly to his native state. Unfortunately, Pierce found peace hard to come by even in the quiet countryside of New Hampshire. He struggled with depression, and neither he nor his wife could get over their grief at the loss of three sons. Pierce never emerged from the shadow of his failed presidency, but he is remembered proudly by his home state. The Pierce home in Hillsborough County, New Hampshire, is now a historic landmark, and a local college and law school bear his name.

With the Union my best and dearest earthly hopes are entwined. Without it, what are we individually or collectively? What becomes of the noblest field ever opened for the advancement of our race in religion, in government, in the arts, and in all that dignifies and adorns mankind? From that radiant constellation that both illumines our own way and points out to struggling nations their course, let but a single star be lost, and, if these not be utter darkness, the luster of the whole is dimmed. . . . It is with me an earnest and vital belief that as the Union had been the source, under Providence, of our prosperity to this time, so it is the surest pledge of a continuance of the blessings we have enjoyed and which we are sacredly bound to transmit undiminished to our children.

from Franklin Pierce's Inaugural Address, delivered March 4, 1853, entirely from memory

JAMES BUCHANAN
1791–1868
FIFTEENTH PRESIDENT 1857–1861

The last president to serve before the Civil War, James Buchanan, like those that came before him, was powerless to calm the anger of the divided American people. A lifelong public servant and avowed optimist, Buchanan took on the presidency with high hopes, but he left with words of foreboding for his successor, Abraham Lincoln: "My dear sir," Buchanan remarked to the sixteenth president, "if you are as happy on entering the White House as I am on leaving, you are a very happy man indeed."

Born in 1791 in Cove Gap, Pennsylvania, Buchanan received an early education from his mother, who loved literature and poetry and often had her children memorize passages from Milton. He went to college at Dickinson in Carlisle, Pennsylvania, and later to law school. After a few years as a lawyer, Buchanan began a string of elected and appointed offices, including seats in the House and Senate as well as appointments as minister to Russia and Great Britain and secretary of state. He won the presidency in 1856, running on a platform of conciliation; and he took office convinced that he could avert civil war by working a compromise between North and South.

Buchanan, the only American president never to marry, had no natural children but did raise an orphaned niece, Harriet Lane, whom he took with him to the White House to serve as official hostess. Their time in Washington was marked by turmoil. The president supported the Supreme Court's controversial Dred Scott decision, which declared that blacks were not citizens and therefore not entitled to the rights guaranteed by the Constitution. Buchanan believed that this decision supported his own view that slavery was protected by the Constitution, and he continued to work toward compromise with this as his foundation. As his term drew to a close, Buchanan stood by as South Carolina seceded from the Union, followed soon thereafter by Alabama, Florida, Georgia, Louisiana, Texas, and Mississippi. Buchanan believed that the federal government had no constitutional authority to force any state to remain in the Union and thus believed himself powerless to act. He left office with the country fractured far beyond the reach of any compromise.

James Buchanan lived a quiet life in retirement and remained, for the most part, on his Wheatland estate in Lancaster, Pennsylvania. He loyally supported the Union during the Civil War and spoke out in favor of President Johnson's post-war efforts at Reconstruction in the South. He died in 1868 at Wheatland.

It may be proper that on this occasion I should make some brief remarks in regard to our rights and duties as a member of the great family of nations. In our intercourse with them there are some plain principles, approved by our own experience from which we should never depart. We ought to cultivate peace, commerce, and friendship with all nations, and this is not merely as the best means of promoting our own interests, but in a spirit of Christian benevolence toward our fellow men, wherever their lot may be cast. Our diplomacy should be direct and frank, neither seeking to obtain more nor accepting less than is our due. We ought to cherish a sacred regard for the independence of all nations, and never attempt to interfere in the domestic concerns of any unless this shall be imperatively required by the great law of self preservation. To avoid entangling alliances has been a maxim of our policy ever since the days of Washington, and its wisdom no one will attempt to dispute. In short, we ought to do justice in a kindly spirit to all nations and require justice from them in return.

from James Buchanan's Inaugural Address, delivered March 4, 1857

James Buchanan was a large, handsome man who had a habit of holding his head cocked to the left, a posture he developed to compensate for the rare eye disorder that left him nearsighted in one eye and farsighted in the other. Depending upon whether he wished to focus on something in close or at a distance, Buchanan would close one eye, cock his head, and look from a single eye. The only bachelor president, Buchanan was engaged at the age of twenty-eight to Anne C. Coleman of Lancaster, Pennsylvania. After a quarrel, however, Miss Coleman left Buchanan and soon thereafter died of an undetermined illness. It was after the death of his one-time fiancée that Buchanan left his law practice and threw himself into public life, hoping to conquer his grief by immersing himself in work.

ABRAHAM LINCOLN
1809–1865
SIXTEENTH PRESIDENT 1861–1865

The story of Abraham Lincoln's life is a true American legend: born in a tiny, one-room log cabin in Kentucky to an illiterate father, he taught himself to read by candlelight and, with the encouragement of a caring stepmother, grew up to be the greatest leader the country has ever known. Lincoln once estimated that he received one year of formal education in his life; but with hard work and perseverance he won election to the Illinois legislature and admittance to the Illinois bar. It was after a successful law career in Illinois and a term as United States Representative that Lincoln set his sights on the White House.

With his heavy frontier accent, down-home wit, and unassuming manner, Abe Lincoln was perhaps an unlikely candidate for the presidency; but his honesty, integrity, deep concern for his fellow man, and fierce commitment to his country won him the confidence of the American people. Lincoln, a veteran of the Black Hawk War, had gained national prominence in an unsuccessful run for the Senate against Stephen Douglas. A series of debates between the two candidates, centering on the issue of slavery, showcased Lincoln's unique flair for public speaking and his passionate commitment to preservation of the Union. Lincoln lost the Senate election but two years later won the presidency and the job of holding together the Union during the Civil War.

For four years the war raged on, claiming countless lives, tearing apart families and friends, threatening the very existence of the nation. Unlike so many leaders of his day, Lincoln seemed always to understand that the Union could not survive half slave and half free, and he eventually came to believe that slavery must be abolished throughout the land. Through it all, Lincoln remained true to what he believed to be his most sacred duty: preserving the Union. In the end, he proved himself equal to the task. The war ended at the start of Lincoln's second term as president with the Union preserved.

Abraham Lincoln was assassinated on April 14, 1865, five days after Lee's surrender at Appomattox. Denied the chance to lead his country in peacetime as he had in war, Lincoln nonetheless left a mark on American history which will never fade. William H. Herndon, Lincoln's law partner, knew him as a friend and as a leader and offered this fitting tribute: "Although he cared little for simple facts, rules and methods, it was on the underlying principle of truth and justice that Lincoln's will was firm as steel and tenacious as iron. . . . When justice, right, liberty, the government, the Constitution, the Union, humanity were involved, then you may all stand aside. No man can move him. No set of men can."

Abraham and Mary Todd Lincoln had four sons. Their third son, William Wallace "Willie" Lincoln, died tragically in the White House in 1862. He was only twelve years old. Lincoln, who was particularly close to Willie, never recovered from his loss; and Mary, never emotionally stable, deteriorated even more after the death of her son. The couple's second son, Edward, and fourth son, Thomas, or Tad, who is pictured with his father at left, died in childhood as well. Robert Todd Lincoln, the family's firstborn, served the Union in the Civil War and went on to become a lawyer like his father.

Abraham Lincoln was born in a one-room log cabin in Hardin County, Kentucky, in February of 1809. When he was two years old, the family moved ten miles north to Knob Creek. In 1816 they moved again, this time to Spencer County, Indiana, where Abe and his father built a 360-square-foot log cabin that would serve as home to Abraham, his sister Sarah, his father, his stepmother, and her four children. Lincoln's mother, Nancy Hanks Lincoln, died when her son was nine years old. Lincoln remembered her fondly all his life; but it was his stepmother, Sarah Bush Lincoln, who was to have the greatest influence on his life, encouraging his attempts at education and self-improvement.

We are now far into the fifth year since a policy was initiated with the avowed object and confident promise of putting an end to slavery agitation. Under the operation of that policy, the agitation has not only not ceased, but has constantly augmented. In my opinion, it will not cease until a crisis shall have been reached and passed. "A house divided against itself cannot stand." (Mark 3:25) I believe this government cannot endure permanently half-slave and half-free. I do not expect the Union to be dissolved; I do not expect the house to fall; but I do expect it will cease to be divided. It will become all one thing, or all the other. Either the opponents of slavery will arrest the further spread of it, and place it where the public mind shall rest in the belief that it is in the course of ultimate extinction, or its advocates will push it forward till it shall become alike lawful in all the States, old as well as new, North as well as South.

from Abraham Lincoln's speech at the Illinois Republican convention of 1858, accepting the nomination to run for Senate against Stephen A. Douglas

Andrew Johnson took an unusual route to the presidency. Not only was he illiterate into adulthood, but at the age of fourteen he was bound as an apprentice to a tailor in Raleigh, North Carolina, an arrangement that called for a term of indentured servitude in exchange for training in the trade. Johnson, however, was not satisfied with his lot in Raleigh, and after only two years he and his brother, also apprenticed to the tailor, ran away. The tailor posted a reward for their return, but the fugitives avoided capture. They settled in Greeneville, Tennessee, where Andrew soon met Eliza McCardle, the young woman who would become his wife and his tutor and thereby start him on the path to the presidency. Eliza and Andrew Johnson had two daughters and three sons, one of whom was killed while serving the Union in the Civil War.

ANDREW JOHNSON
1808–1875
SEVENTEENTH PRESIDENT 1865–1869

Named for former president Andrew Jackson, Andrew Johnson, born in 1808 in Raleigh, North Carolina, came from common, southern roots. Johnson's father, Jacob, alternately a janitor, church sexton, and hotel porter, died when his son was three, leaving Polly Johnson to support the family by taking in spinning and weaving. Johnson received no education in childhood and was the only president to be illiterate into adulthood. He began his career as a tailor in Greeneville, Tennessee. Through the tutoring of his wife, Eliza, whom he married when he was eighteen and she sixteen, Johnson eventually learned to read and won the position of alderman in Greeneville, beginning a career in public service that would lead all the way to the White House.

Stirred by ambition and helped along by a flair for public speaking, Johnson went on from alderman to the Tennessee House of Representatives, the United States House, and in 1853, the office of governor of Tennessee. Johnson was a United States senator when the Civil War began. His support of the president and the Union won him strong disapproval at home but gained the notice of a grateful President Lincoln. In 1862 Lincoln appointed Johnson military governor of Tennessee, with the responsibility of maintaining order and reestablishing federal control. He held that post until 1864, when Lincoln, hoping that a pro-Union southerner would add balance to his bid for reelection, chose him as his vice presidential running mate. The two would serve together only a month before Lincoln was assassinated and Johnson inherited the highest job in the land.

Johnson took the reins of a nation finally at peace but battered by war and shocked by the assassination of its leader. He intended to follow the course of Reconstruction set out by Lincoln but met with opposition from all sides. Southerners resented federal presence in their states, and northerners believed the government was too lenient on the Confederates. The conflict led to Johnson's impeachment. Although he was acquitted of all charges, his presidency never recovered. Despite his weakness in office, however, Johnson made one significant decision. In 1867 he agreed to purchase Alaska from Russia for just over seven million dollars. Considered a wasteland at the time, Alaska is today treasured for its unmatched natural resources and beauty.

Johnson retired to his adopted home state of Tennessee after his term in office. He remained active in public life and, in 1875, won election to the Senate, the only former president to do so. He died in office in 1875 of complications following a bout with cholera.

Slavery is dead, and you must pardon me if I do not mourn over its dead body; you can bury it out of sight. . . . I desire that all men shall have a fair start and an equal chance in the race of life, and let him succeed who has the most merit. I am for emancipation, for two reasons: first, because it is right in itself; and second, because in the emancipation of the slaves we break down an odious and dangerous aristocracy. I think that we are freeing more whites than blacks.

President Andrew Johnson speaking in Nashville, Tennessee, at the close of the Civil War

ULYSSES S. GRANT
1822–1885
EIGHTEENTH PRESIDENT 1869–1877

Born in 1822 in Point Pleasant, Ohio, Ulysses S. Grant showed no signs in childhood of being a future military hero. A slight, quiet child, Ulysses loved horses, not war games, and he was too sensitive even to help out his father in the elder Grant's tanning shop. Following his father's wishes, however, Grant entered West Point, where he was an average student, excelling in horsemanship and math but struggling with military science.

After graduating from West Point—closer to the bottom than the top of his class—Grant received his commission and began a lifelong career as a soldier. He served first in the Mexican War, after which he married Julia Boggs Dent, a match that went against the wishes of both families. The abolitionist Grants disapproved of the slaveholding Dents; and the Dents, with high hopes for their daughter, saw little promise in the young Mr. Grant.

The Dents were to be proven wrong during the Civil War, which Grant began as an infantry colonel and finished as the commander of the Union Army. Displaying great bravery and undying commitment to the Union, Grant became a national hero. It was he who, in 1865, accepted the surrender of General Lee at Appomattox, showing the same grace in victory that he had in battle. After the war, President Lincoln promoted Grant to General of the Army. He was the first American to hold this post since George Washington.

Due to his unrivaled popularity with the American people, Grant was the obvious and unopposed choice of the Republican party for president in 1868. He neither campaigned nor made promises. With the simple slogan "Let us have peace," Grant won a convincing electoral victory to become the eighteenth president. Inexperienced and unprepared for the demands of the presidency, however, Grant was an ineffective chief executive. Rocked by scandal, he struggled with the continuing problems of Reconstruction, which were compounded by a lengthy depression. Nonetheless, Grant, still a national hero, won reelection and served two full terms in office.

In retirement, Grant traveled the globe, wrote his memoirs, and struggled through great financial hardship. He died in 1885 in New York. His final resting place, Grant's Tomb, is now a monument overlooking New York's Hudson River.

Ulysses S. Grant lived in this brick home in Galena, Illinois, for a short time after his retirement from public life. Grant left the White House in 1877 and, with his wife and son Jesse, embarked upon an extended trip throughout Europe, Asia, and Africa. When he returned to the United States, Grant moved to Galena but soon found himself again a leading candidate for the Republican presidential nomination. Grant eventually lost the nomination to James Garfield and sold the home in Galena to move to New York City, where he spent the remainder of his retirement.

Ulysses S. Grant was born as Hiram Ulysses Grant. When he enrolled at West Point, he reversed his first and middle names to avoid having the initials H. U. G. engraved on his trunk. Due to a mistake on his enrollment forms, however, Grant became known in school records and forever after as Ulysses Simpson Grant. The former president and his family are pictured here on the porch of their New York home shortly before his death in 1885. Grant and his wife Julia, despite the objections of their families, married in 1848 and went on to have four children, Frederick Dent Grant, Ulysses S. Grant, Jr., Ellen Wrenshall Grant, and Jesse Root Grant. Ellen, known as Nellie, was married at the White House in 1874.

Your suffrage having elected me to the office of the President of the United States, I have, in conformity to the Constitution of our country, taken the oath of office prescribed therein. I have taken this oath without mental reservation and with the determination to do to the best of my ability all that is required of me. The responsibilities of the position I feel, but accept them without fear. The office has come to me unsought; I commence its duties untrammeled. I bring to it a conscious desire and determination to fill it to the best of my ability to the satisfaction of the people.

On all the leading questions agitating the public mind I will always express my views to Congress and urge them according to my judgment, and when I think it advisable will exercise the constitutional privilege of interposing vetoes to defeat measures which I oppose; but all laws will be faithfully executed, whether they meet my approval or not.

I shall on all subjects have a policy to recommend, but none to enforce against the will of the people. Laws are to govern all alike—those opposed as well as those who favor them. I know no method to secure the repeal of bad or obnoxious laws so effective as their stringent execution.

The country having just emerged from a great rebellion, many questions will come before it for settlement in the next four years which preceding Administrations have never had to deal with. In meeting these it is desirable that they should be approached calmly, without prejudice, hate, or sectional pride, remembering the greatest good to the greatest number is the object to be attained.

*from Ulysses S. Grant's first Inaugural Address,
delivered March 4, 1869*

RUTHERFORD B. HAYES
1822–1893
NINETEENTH PRESIDENT 1877–1881

A sturdy man with a long, full beard, Rutherford Birchard Hayes was a cheerful extrovert whose love of people made him perfectly suited for public office. He was born in Delaware, Ohio, in 1822, shortly after the death of his father. The greatest influence on his youth was his older sister, Fanny, with whom he remained close throughout his life.

After graduating from Harvard Law School, Hayes settled back home in Ohio to practice law. His career was interrupted, however, by four years' service in the Union army during the Civil War. Hayes returned from the war a hero and, before he could resume his law practice, found himself nominated for a seat in the Ohio House of Representatives. Although he did not actively campaign, Hayes was elected on his war record and began a rise through the ranks of Ohio politics that would culminate in his election as governor. It was from the governor's office that Hayes, now convinced that politics and not law was his calling, launched his run for the White House in 1876. In an election so close that Hayes went to bed on election night believing himself the loser, the Ohio governor became the nineteenth president.

As president, Hayes fulfilled his election promise and formally put an end to Reconstruction with the Compromise of 1877, which called for the final withdrawal of all federal troops from the South. Hayes also laid the foundation for the construction of an American-controlled canal across the Isthmus of Panama. In response to European intentions to build a canal through Central America, President Hayes vowed to Congress that any canal built in the region would be constructed and controlled by the United States. The Panama Canal would not be built for another quarter century, but Hayes's pledge of American control was to be fulfilled.

Before his election, Rutherford Hayes announced his desire to be a single-term president. He remained true to his word, retiring in 1881 with his wife, Lucy, to Spiegel Grove, his Ohio estate. Mrs. Hayes died in 1889, four years before her husband. Both are buried at Spiegel Grove.

Let me assure my countrymen of the southern states that it is my earnest desire to regard and promote their truest interest—the interests of the white and of the colored people both and equally—and to put forth my best efforts in behalf of a civil policy which will forever wipe out in our political affairs the color line and the distinction between North and South, to the end that we may have not merely a united North or a united South, but a united country.

from Rutherford B. Hayes's Inaugural Address, delivered March 5, 1877

In 1877 the White House was the site of a special celebration in honor of President Rutherford and Lucy Hayes's twenty-fifth wedding anniversary. Mrs. Hayes, the mother of five children, had been a visible first lady. A devout Methodist, she banned all alcoholic beverages in the White House and held regular hymn sings for Washington officials. Lucy Hayes also initiated the beloved annual White House Easter Egg Roll. A portrait of Mrs. Hayes, commissioned by the Women's Christian Temperance Union, hangs in the White House to this day.

The last president to be born in a log cabin, James Garfield had a wide range of experience in his life before the presidency, including a stint as a canal boat driver, a position that gave him responsibility for leading the mules that pulled boats through the canal. Garfield hung onto life for almost three months after being shot at the Baltimore and Potomac Railroad station in Washington, D.C., in July of 1881. The latest medical technology was used in an attempt to save the president, including an electronic device supposedly capable of finding the location of the bullet in the president's body. The device, which was used to no avail, was operated by Alexander Graham Bell, inventor of the telephone.

JAMES A. GARFIELD
1831–1881
TWENTIETH PRESIDENT 1881

As a child in Orange Township, Ohio, James Abram Garfield dreamed of being a sailor, not of becoming president of the United States. After a brief time aboard an Ohio canal boat, however, Garfield discovered himself ill-suited to life on the water and turned his attention to his education. Determined to succeed in school despite limited family finances, Garfield worked as a janitor, a carpenter, and a teacher to support himself through local private schools and Williams College in Massachusetts.

It was at Williams that Garfield heard a speech by Ralph Waldo Emerson that inspired him to leave his mark upon the world. After graduation, he taught classical languages for a time; but bored with the quiet life of a teacher, he later took up the study of law. Upon admittance to the bar in 1860, Garfield was already a state senator. Three years later he began a term in the United States House of Representatives that would last until 1880, when he sought and won the presidency.

James A. Garfield was shot on July 2, 1881, not quite four months after his inauguration. He survived two months, finally giving up his life on September 19. His assassin was Charles J. Guiteau, a former supporter bitter because the president had passed him over for a diplomatic post.

Garfield had little time to accomplish much as president, and what time he did have was consumed by a scandal at the post office. Perhaps his most lasting contribution was the impetus his assassination gave to devising a less partisan means of awarding government jobs. Garfield was on his way to visit his wife, Lucretia, recovering from malaria in New Jersey, when he was shot. After the president's death, Lucretia and their five children settled in Ohio.

The supreme trial of the Constitution came at last under the tremendous pressure of civil war. We ourselves are witnesses that the Union emerged from the blood and fire of that conflict purified and made stronger for all the beneficent purposes of good government. . . . the nation is resolutely facing to the front, resolved to employ its best energies in developing the great possibilities of the future. Sacredly preserving whatever has been gained to liberty and good government during the century, our people are determined to leave behind them all those bitter controversies concerning things which have been irrevocably settled, and the further discussion of which can only stir up strife and delay the onward march.

The supremacy of the nation and its laws should no longer be a subject of debate. That discussion, which for half a century threatened the existence of the Union, was closed at last in the high court of war by a decree from which there is no appeal—that the Constitution and the laws made in pursuance thereof are and shall continue to be the supreme law of the land, binding alike upon the States and the people. This decree does not disturb the autonomy of the States nor interfere with any of their necessary rights of local self-government, but it does fix and establish the permanent supremacy of the Union.

The will of the nation, speaking with the voice of battle and through the amended Constitution, has fulfilled the great promise of 1776 by proclaiming "liberty throughout the land to all the inhabitants thereof."

from James A. Garfield's Inaugural Address, delivered March 4, 1881

CHESTER A. ARTHUR
1829–1886
TWENTY-FIRST PRESIDENT 1881–1885

Chester A. Arthur was elected to only one office during his life, that of vice president under James A. Garfield in 1880. His only other public office was the appointed post of collector of the port of New York. Arthur became president in September of 1881 after the assassination of President Garfield.

For most of his career, Arthur practiced law in New York. His most famous case was that of Lizzie Jennings, a black woman who filed suit against a New York street car company after being refused a seat on a "whites only" train. Arthur won the case for Ms. Jennings and forced the eventual desegregation of all public street cars in New York City.

As president, Arthur worked with Congress on civil service reform, an issue which became a priority after the backlash of the longstanding spoils system— the policy of awarding government jobs based on political connections—led to the assassination of President Garfield. Although Arthur himself had benefitted from the spoils system earlier in his career—his political connections won him the lucrative and much sought-after position of collector of the port of New York—he signed into law the Pendleton Act of 1883, which provided for civil service exams, put an end to enforced political contributions for government employees, and discouraged nepotism. Arthur intended to seek a second term as president, but the Republican party felt he had gone too far in his efforts to reform the federal government and refused to give him a second nomination.

Chester Arthur was a Vermont native from a family of devout Baptists. He was renowned for his full mustache and side-whiskers and his tall, heavy-set build. His wife, Nell, died before her husband became president, and left him with the care of their son and daughter. Arthur himself died in 1886, at the age of fifty-six, of Bright's Disease, a kidney ailment that had troubled him since his days as president.

Men may die, but the fabrics of our free institutions remain unshaken. No higher or more assuring proof could exist of the strength and the permanence of popular government than the fact that though the chosen of the people be struck down, his constitutional successor is peacefully installed without shock or strain, except the sorrow which mourns the bereavement.

Chester A. Arthur, speaking after the death of President Garfield in 1881

Chester Arthur was born in this small house in Fairfield, Vermont, but throughout his childhood moved continually across Vermont and New York State as his father, a Baptist preacher, moved from church to church. The Reverend William Arthur was a passionate, outspoken man, an ardent abolitionist who came to America from Ireland by way of Quebec as a young man. Arthur's mother, Malvina Stone, was also a devout Baptist. Chester Arthur, however, never accepted his parents' faith. He attended Episcopalian services with his wife, Nell, and continued to do so after her death; he never formally joined a church.

GROVER CLEVELAND

1837–1908

TWENTY-SECOND PRESIDENT 1885–1889
TWENTY-FOURTH PRESIDENT 1893–1897

The only president to be elected to two non-consecutive terms, Grover Cleveland was an ambitious, hard-working man who took his responsibilities as president as the most serious commitment in his life.

Cleveland, born in New Jersey and raised in Clinton, New York, credited his success in life to his strict Presbyterian upbringing, which taught him the importance of faith and self-discipline. An ambitious student, Cleveland had hopes of attending college, but when his father, a minister, died in 1853, Cleveland put aside thoughts of higher education and set out toward Ohio, where he hoped to find work. He stopped along the way in Buffalo, New York, and went to work for an uncle who was a successful stock breeder. In his spare time, Cleveland began to study law. Six years later, still in Buffalo, Cleveland won admittance to the New York bar and began working as a lawyer, with aspirations of entering politics. His rise to the presidency began in 1882 with his election as mayor of Buffalo. The Cleveland administration was so immediately successful and popular that community leaders urged their mayor to run for governor. He won that job in 1882 and within two years was the Democratic nominee for the office of president.

In his first term in the White House, Cleveland worked to reduce tariffs on imported goods in hopes of increasing foreign trade. The tariff issue was being debated throughout America, and Cleveland's stand was a generally unpopular one. Most Americans believed that free trade would damage domestic industry. When Cleveland stood for reelection four years later, he was narrowly defeated by Benjamin Harrison, who assuaged their fears with promises to protect American industry from foreign competition. Defeated but not discouraged, Cleveland returned to his law practice in Buffalo. Four years later he challenged Harrison and won a second chance at the presidency.

Back in the White House, after his four-year hiatus, Cleveland continued to push for lower tariffs, this time sure to insist that he was not in favor of absolute free trade. He also faced two major crises: the Panic of 1893 and the Pullman Strike in Chicago. Cleveland believed that the Panic, which was the result of a major railroad failure and led to a serious four-year depression, must be solved with a return to the gold standard. In the famous Pullman Strike, railroad workers in Chicago formed a union and shut down rail service between their city and the Pacific. Cleveland acted decisively and swiftly, using federal authority to end the strike.

In retirement, Cleveland moved to Princeton, New Jersey, where he was active for the remainder of his life in the affairs of Princeton University. He also wrote several articles for the *Saturday Evening Post,* one of which detailed a secret operation performed while he was president to remove a cancerous part of his jaw. In surgery that took place on a boat on New York's East River—to avoid public notice—Cleveland had a rubber jaw implanted and his cancer effectively cured. Cleveland died in 1908, leaving four young children and his wife, Frances, whom he had married at the White House when she was only twenty-one. Frances Cleveland lived another thirty-nine years. She later remarried and during the Great Depression won the hearts of the American people by leading a drive to collect clothing for the poor.

Grover Cleveland was a large, impos- ing figure, weighing over two hundred and fifty pounds and standing just short of six feet tall. He was a bachelor when first elected president, but in June of 1886 he married twenty-one- year-old Frances Folsom in the first- ever White House wedding ceremony for a president. The ceremony, per- formed in the Blue Room, was small and simple, with musical accompani- ment by John Philip Sousa and the Marine Band. Seven years later, dur- ing the second Cleveland administra- tion, the first family achieved another presidential first with the birth of Esther Cleveland, the only child to be born to a president in the White House.

He who takes the oath today to preserve, protect, and defend the Constitution of the United States, only assumes the solemn obligation which every patriotic citizen—on the farm, in the workshop, in the busy marts of trade, and everywhere—should share with him. The Constitution which prescribes this oath, my countrymen, is yours; the suffrage which executes the will of freemen is yours; the laws and the entire scheme of our civil rule, from the town meeting to the State capitals and the national capital, is yours.

. . . Every citizen owes to the country a vigilant watch and close scrutiny of its public servants and a fair and reasonable estimate of their fidelity and usefulness. Thus is the people's will impressed upon the whole framework of our civil polity—municipal, state, and federal; and this is the price of our liberty and inspiration of our faith in the Republic.

from Grover Cleveland's first Inaugural Address, delivered March 4, 1885

Benjamin Harrison defeated Grover Cleveland to win the presidency in 1888 despite the fact that Cleveland received forty-nine percent of the popular vote to Harrison's forty-eight. The difference was in the electoral votes, specifically in Cleveland's electoral-rich home state of New York, which he failed to win. Four years later, the same two candidates squared off again in the national election. This time, in another close race, Cleveland emerged victorious in both the popular and electoral votes. Although the two men differed greatly on the important issue of tariffs, their two campaigns were, in the words of a political observer, marked by "decency and dignity."

BENJAMIN HARRISON
1833–1901
TWENTY-THIRD PRESIDENT 1889–1893

The twenty-third president, Benjamin Harrison, was born with American politics in his blood. His great-grandfather signed the Declaration of Independence and his grandfather, William Henry Harrison, was the ninth president. He was not, however, born a natural politician. Stiff and often cold with people, Harrison succeeded by virtue of hard work, integrity, and intelligence.

Born on his grandfather's farm in North Bend, Ohio, Benjamin was a bright and motivated student. He graduated from Miami University in Ohio in 1852 and embarked upon a career in law. His legal career was interrupted by three years' service in the Civil War, during which he rose to the rank of brigadier general. After the war, Harrison continued his law practice until 1881, when he began a term representing his adopted home state of Indiana in the United States Senate. Harrison remained in the Senate until 1888, when he defeated Grover Cleveland to become the twenty-third president.

In office, Harrison signed into law the Dependent and Disability Pensions Act, which improved compensation to disabled veterans. In direct opposition to Grover Cleveland, who had served before him and would again serve after him, Harrison supported an act to require the U.S. government to purchase silver from western mines. He believed this would increase the amount of money in circulation and thus stimulate the economy. Harrison, a protectionist, also disagreed with Cleveland's stand on tariffs, and during the Harrison administration the tariff on imported goods rose to forty-eight percent. Both the Silver Purchase Act and the new tariff were overridden by measures in the second Cleveland administration. Harrison ran for reelection but lost to the same man he had defeated four years earlier, Grover Cleveland.

Benjamin Harrison married Caroline Lavinia Scott in 1853. During her husband's term as president, Mrs. Harrison supervised expensive renovations at the White House, including the installation of modern plumbing and electricity. Although she was in favor of bringing electricity to the White House, Mrs. Harrison was reportedly afraid to touch the switches and had employees turn them on in the morning and off again at night. Caroline died during her husband's campaign for reelection. In retirement, Harrison married Mary Dimmick, a niece of his first wife. They lived in Indianapolis until the former president's death in 1901.

Two presidents or three, with equal powers, would as surely bring disaster as three generals of equal rank and command in a single army. I do not doubt that this sense of single and personal responsibility to the people has strongly held our presidents to a good conscience, and to a high discharge of their duties.

Benjamin Harrison, writing on the presidency in 1897

WILLIAM MCKINLEY
1843–1901
TWENTY-FIFTH PRESIDENT 1897–1901

William McKinley campaigned for the presidency in 1897 without leaving his home in Canton, Ohio. In his "front porch" campaign, McKinley spoke daily to large gatherings outside his home but left the hard work of the campaign trail to a devoted group of supporters who spread out across the country on behalf of their candidate. McKinley's strategy worked. In 1897 he became the twenty-fifth president of the United States.

McKinley did not remain at home during the campaign due to any reticence on his part, for he was an outgoing, friendly man with a real gift for storytelling and public speaking. Humble, yet confident, McKinley was popular with supporters and opponents alike. He was born in Niles, Ohio, and from his own reports was a happy, active child who found early success at his Methodist high school as a founding member of the debating club.

Family finances and the Civil War prevented McKinley from attending college, but after the war he worked for a Youngstown, Ohio, judge and studied law. He became a lawyer in 1867 and soon gained the notice of the local Republican party, which urged him to run for the House of Representatives in 1877. McKinley served a total of fourteen years in the House, where he became known as a fervent supporter of protectionism. He left the House in 1891 to become governor of Ohio and, in 1896, ran successfully against William Jennings Bryan for the presidency.

In his first term as president McKinley led the nation into the Spanish-American War with the goal of establishing stability and independence in Cuba. The war resulted in the acquisition of the Philippines, Puerto Rico, and Guam as United States territories and freed Cuba from Spanish control. McKinley also negotiated the annexation of Hawaii and, in the continuing battle between free trade advocates and protectionists, restored a high tariff on imported goods in hopes of boosting domestic industry. McKinley won a second term in 1900 but served only six more months before Leon F. Czolgosz, an unemployed Detroit millworker, assassinated him in Buffalo, New York. Czolgosz, an anarchist, shot the president because he believed him to be "an enemy of the people."

McKinley was survived by his wife Ida, who had already suffered with her husband the tragedy of losing two infant daughters. Mrs. McKinley, to whom the president had been extremely devoted, died only six years after her husband's assassination.

President McKinley was assassinated at the 1901 Pan American Exposition in Buffalo, New York, as he shook hands in a receiving line at the Temple of Music. As his assassin, Leon Czolgosz approached, McKinley held out his hand. Czolgosz extended a bandaged hand in which was concealed his gun. After two shots were fired and the president fell to the floor, Secret Service agents rushed at Czolgosz. McKinley, seeing his assassin surrounded, cried out to the crowd in a strange moment of concern for his attacker, "Don't let them hurt him!"

In conclusion, I congratulate the country upon the fraternal spirit of the people and the manifestations of good will everywhere so apparent. The recent election not only most fortunately demonstrated the obliteration of sectional or geographical lines, but to some extent also the prejudices which for years have distracted our councils and marred our true greatness as a nation. The triumph of the people, whose verdict is carried into effect today, is not the triumph of one section, nor wholly of one party, but of all sections and all the people. The North and the South no longer divide on the old lines, but upon principles and policies; and in this fact surely every lover of the country can find cause for true felicitation. Let us rejoice in and cultivate this spirit; it is ennobling and will be both a gain and a blessing to our beloved country. It will be my constant aim to do nothing, and permit nothing to be done, that will arrest or disturb this growing sentiment of unity and cooperation, this revival of esteem and affiliation which now animate so many thousands in both the old antagonistic sections, but I shall cheerfully do everything possible to promote and increase it.

from William McKinley's Inaugural Address, delivered March 4, 1897

THEODORE ROOSEVELT
1858–1919
TWENTY-SIXTH PRESIDENT 1901–1909

Born in New York City in 1858 to a family of great wealth, Theodore Roosevelt was a sickly child, too weak for sports or outdoor recreation. By adulthood, however, through a devoted course of physical activity, Roosevelt had grown into a robust, energetic man, fond of hiking, boxing, swimming, and tennis and ready to take on any challenge life could offer.

Roosevelt graduated Phi Beta Kappa from Harvard and went on to Columbia Law School but, in 1881, left school to run for the New York State Assembly. He won three consecutive terms in the Assembly, where his youth and energy earned him a quick reputation. Roosevelt had found his life's calling in politics, but still full of the spirit of youth and grieving over the sudden death of his wife, Alice, he left New York for the Dakota Territory, where he worked as a cattle rancher and a deputy sheriff. In 1886 Roosevelt returned to New York and began his rise to the White House, serving as U.S. Civil Service commissioner, police commissioner of New York City, as secretary of the navy, and as governor of New York. Roosevelt also served in the Spanish-American War, winning fame as leader of the Rough Riders, the volunteer cavalry regiment that led the U.S. charge up San Juan Hill in Cuba. Roosevelt became vice president in 1901 and, six months later, upon the death of President McKinley, he acceded to the presidency.

For eight years, Theodore Roosevelt sat at the helm of the nation as it began the twentieth century, acting boldly and aggressively but also fairly and intelligently. He took up the cause of maintaining stability in Latin America, using U.S. power to enforce what he called "big stick" diplomacy. Roosevelt also presided over the planning of the Panama Canal and became known as a "trust buster" for his work to end large corporate monopolies. One of the most lasting legacies of the Roosevelt administration is its spirit of conservationism. A lover of the outdoors, Teddy Roosevelt did much to preserve the nation's natural beauty and resources. In 1906 he won the Nobel Peace Prize for his work toward peace between Russia and Japan.

Married twice—his first wife, Alice, died after only three years of marriage whereas his second wife, Edith, outlived him by almost thirty years—Roosevelt

Vice President Theodore Roosevelt was hunting in New York's Adirondack Mountains when he received word that President McKinley was close to death. Roosevelt left camp immediately, descending a dark mountain road in record time to reach Buffalo, New York, one day later, on September 14, 1901. McKinley died that day, and Roosevelt took the oath of office to become president. He wrote of his sudden promotion: "It is a dreadful thing to come into the presidency this way; but it would be a far worse thing to become morbid about it. Here is the task, and I have got to do it to the best of my ability."

was father to six children and enjoyed their company immensely. He never lost his love of the active life or his enthusiasm for public service. Upon retirement in 1909, Roosevelt embarked upon an African safari and a tour of Europe. The remainder of his retirement was no less active, including more trips abroad and continued involvement in politics. Roosevelt died in 1919 at Sagamore Hill, his estate on Long Island.

Close to death, Theodore Roosevelt is said to have remarked to his wife, "I wonder if you will ever know how much I love Sagamore Hill." The family estate at Oyster Bay on Long Island, New York, Sagamore Hill was the center of the large, active, and loving Roosevelt family. Even as president, Roosevelt delighted in playing with his children, and he encouraged them to be as full of life as he was. The six young Roosevelts heeded their father's wishes and filled the White House with their games and mischief. Asked about his precocious, free-spirited eldest daughter, Alice, Roosevelt once replied, "I can be president of the United States or I can control Alice. I cannot do both."

I preach to you, then, my countrymen, that our country calls not for the life of ease, but for the life of strenuous endeavor. The twentieth century looms before us big with the fate of many nations. If we stand idly by, if we seek merely swollen, slothful ease, and ignoble peace, if we shrink from the hard contests where men must win at hazard of their lives and at the risk of all they hold dear, then the bolder and stronger peoples will pass us by and will win for themselves the domination of the world. Let us therefore boldly face the life of strife, resolute to do our duty well and manfully; resolute to uphold righteousness by deed and by word; resolute to be both honest and brave, to serve high ideals, yet to use practical methods. Above all, let us shrink from no strife, moral or physical, within or without the nation, provided we are certain that the strife is justified; for it is only through strife, through hard and dangerous endeavor, that we shall ultimately win the goal of true national greatness.

from a speech delivered April 10, 1899, in Chicago while Roosevelt was governor of New York

WILLIAM HOWARD TAFT
1857–1930
TWENTY-SEVENTH PRESIDENT 1909–1913

Distinguished by a handlebar mustache and a weight often more than three hundred pounds, Secretary of War William Howard Taft won the endorsement of outgoing president Theodore Roosevelt in his bid for the presidency in 1908. Pledging to continue the policies of his predecessor and close friend, Taft went on to win the election over William Jennings Bryan and became the twenty-seventh president.

Taft was born in 1857 in Cincinnati, Ohio. His father was a leader in the Republican party and a career diplomat. His mother, Louise Torrey Taft, came from a prominent Boston family. Taft had a happy, active, comfortable childhood. After attending Yale University, where he graduated second in his class, he studied law at the University of Cincinnati, with hopes of following his father into government service. Taft worked in the Cincinnati legal community for twenty years before making his entry into national politics.

In 1900 President McKinley chose Taft to be governor general of the Philippines. On the islands, newly acquired in the Spanish-American War, Taft was to oversee the establishment of a stable government. Taft left the Philippines in 1904, when President Roosevelt called upon him to fill the post of secretary of war. From there, four years later, he made his bid for the White House.

As president, Taft became known for his "dollar diplomacy," a policy which relied upon American industry investments to promote stability in Latin America. Taft also followed through on the anti-trust policies of Theodore Roosevelt, continuing the move to break up and prevent large corporate monopolies.

Taft's wife, Nellie, made her own lasting impression on the city of Washington when she arranged for the planting of three thousand Japanese cherry trees along the Tidal Basin. The annual celebration of the cherry blossoms remains one of Washington's most cherished traditions. Taft himself began another longstanding tradition, that of the president throwing out the first ball to open the professional baseball season.

Taft ran for reelection but found himself opposed not just by the strong Democratic candidate Woodrow Wilson but also by old friend Theodore Roosevelt, who felt that Taft had turned conservative and backed away from his pledge to continue Roosevelt's legacy. The close three-way race went to Wilson.

Despite his defeat, Taft was not disillusioned with public life. After several years as a professor of law at Yale, he accepted appointment as chief justice of the Supreme Court, becoming the only president to hold that position. He served on the court until his death in 1930. Alongside his wife, Nellie, with whom he had three children, William Howard Taft is buried at Arlington National Cemetery. He was the first former president so honored and has since been joined only by John F. Kennedy.

The progress which the Negro has made in the last fifty years, from slavery, when its statistics are reviewed, is marvelous, and it furnishes every reason to hope that in the next twenty-five years a still greater improvement in his condition as a productive member of society . . . may come.

The Negroes are now Americans. Their ancestors came here years ago against their will, and this is their only country and their only flag. They have shown themselves anxious to live for it and to die for it. Encountering the race feelings against them, subjected at times to cruel injustice growing out of it, they may well have our profound sympathy and aid in the struggle they are making. We are charged with the sacred duty of making their path as smooth and as easy as we can.

from William Howard Taft's Inaugural Address, delivered March 4, 1909

William Howard Taft and his family moved into the White House in 1909 with great expectations. Mrs. Taft enjoyed public life and looked forward to much entertaining as first lady. She redecorated much of the house with furniture from their days in the Philippines and filled every room with flowers and plants. The Tafts were the first to have a presidential automobile and the last to keep their own cows. But life in the White House was not to be what the Tafts expected. Not long after Taft's inauguration, Nellie suffered a serious stroke and had to give up all plans for entertaining as she worked to regain normal movement and speech. Taft's health also suffered under the burden of his presidential responsibilities. His weight, always a problem, reached new heights, damaging his public image. When they left the White House after a single term, the Tafts were as glad to be leaving Pennsylvania Avenue as they had been to arrive.

WOODROW WILSON

1856–1924
TWENTY-EIGHTH PRESIDENT 1913–1921

Woodrow Wilson dreamed all his life of a career in politics. The son of a Presbyterian minister and a devoutly religious man who included prayer as a part of his daily routine, Wilson grew to realize his dream and to become one of the great leaders of the twentieth century.

Born in Staunton, Virginia, but raised mostly in Augusta, Georgia, Wilson was troubled by illness and poor eyesight in childhood. Nonetheless, he managed to earn a spot at the College of New Jersey (now known as Princeton University). From there he continued on to law school at the University of Virginia.

Wilson never enjoyed his legal studies but kept at them as a means of entering politics. After graduation, however, he found the practice of law unfulfilling and for a time gave up his political ambitions to pursue higher education and a career as a professor. Wilson earned a Ph.D. in political science at Johns Hopkins, the only president to do so, and worked several years as a professor and scholar before becoming president of Princeton in 1902. Wilson set his alma mater on a course to become one of the leading universities in America before, once again caught up in his dreams of a political career, he left to run for governor of New Jersey. After two successful years as governor, Wilson received the Democratic presidential nomination.

Woodrow Wilson quickly proved himself a skilled leader. Among the early achievements of his administration were the Federal Reserve Act, which created a system of regional, federal banks to provide a measure of stability to the economy; the Federal Trade Commission, created to keep watch over interstate trade; and the Adamson Act, the first step toward the establishment of the eight-hour workday. President Wilson will always be best remembered, however, for his leadership during the First World War. With his pledge to help make the world "safe for democracy," Wilson reluctantly but confidently led American forces into the war in 1917, never losing sight of peace as his ultimate objective. In 1919 he went to Versailles, where he was a leader in the negotiations toward the Treaty of Versailles, which ended the war. With peace secured, Wilson campaigned passionately for the creation of the League of Nations, which he hoped would avert future world conflicts. Woodrow Wilson won the 1919 Nobel Peace Prize for his work promoting world peace.

After two terms as president, Wilson retired to his home in Washington, D.C. His health had been failing ever since he suffered a stroke in the autumn of 1919. Wilson died in 1924 in Washington.

First Lady Edith Wilson, pictured at left with President Wilson, screened all business and visitors for the president after his stroke; she remained by his side and was discreetly instrumental in the running of the government during the president's illness. She was Wilson's second wife. His first, Ellen, with whom he had three daughters, died during his first term in office.

The world must be made safe for democracy. Its peace must be planted upon the tested foundation of political liberty. We have no selfish ends to serve. We desire no conquest, no dominion. We seek no indemnities for ourselves, no material compensation for the sacrifices we shall freely make. We are but one of the champions of the rights of mankind. We shall be satisfied when those rights have been made as secure as the faith and the freedom of nations can make them. . . .There are, it may be, many months of fiery trial and sacrifice ahead of us. It is a fearful thing to lead this great peaceful people into war, into the most terrible and disastrous of all wars, civilization itself seeming to be in the balance. But the right is more precious than peace, and we shall fight for the things which we have always carried nearest our hearts—for democracy, for the right of those who submit to authority to have a voice in their own governments, for the rights and liberties of small nations, for a universal dominion of right by such a concert of free peoples as shall bring peace and safety to all nations and make the world itself at last free. To such a task we can dedicate our lives and our fortunes, everything that we are and everything that we have, with the pride of those who know that the day has come when America is privileged to spend her blood and her might for the principles that gave her birth and happiness and the peace which she has treasured. God helping her, she can do no other.

from Woodrow Wilson's war message to Congress, delivered April 2, 1917, asking Congress for a declaration of war after German submarines sank an American merchant vessel

WARREN G. HARDING
1865–1923
TWENTY-NINTH PRESIDENT 1921–1923

The son of two doctors, Warren Gamaliel Harding grew up on an Ohio farm and learned his early lessons from *McGuffey's Eclectic Readers* in a one-room schoolhouse in a town called Blooming Grove. He began his career not as a politician but as a newspaper editor and publisher in Marion, Ohio.

Harding was born in 1865 in Corsica, Ohio. At fifteen, he left the one-room schoolhouse in Blooming Grove to attend Ohio Central College in Iberia. It was there that he got his start in publishing as the editor of the campus paper. After graduation, Harding continued to work in the newspaper business, eventually buying the *Marion Star* and turning it into a popular and profitable paper.

Harding's ascension to the White House began in the Ohio State Senate in 1899, and he went on to become lieutenant governor of Ohio and a United States senator. Harding won the 1920 Republican nomination for president late in the balloting at the party convention.

In the White House, Harding struggled to live up to the distinguished record of his predecessor, Woodrow Wilson. Scandal troubled his administration almost from the start as members of his cabinet were found guilty of accepting bribes and selling government oil reserves for personal gain. Harding also let the work Wilson had done to form the League of Nations go to waste by refusing to back American membership.

On the positive side, Harding did speak out against discrimination in the South, demanding equal rights for blacks at a speech at the University of Alabama. Nothing he could do, however, would lift the black cloud of scandal from his administration.

Warren Harding died in office in 1923 of what is believed to have been complications of high blood pressure. His wife of thirty-two years, Florence "Flossie" Harding, died sixteen months later. Historians generally agree that Harding was our least successful president.

Mankind needs a world-wide benediction of understanding. It is needed among individuals, among peoples, among governments, and it will inaugurate an era of good feeling. . . . In such understanding men will strive confidently for the promotion of their better relationships and nations will promote the comities so essential to peace.

from Warren G. Harding's Inaugural Address, delivered March 4, 1921

Florence "Flossie" Mabel Kling De Wolfe was thirty years old when she married Warren Harding in 1891 in Marion, Ohio. It was her second marriage. Mrs. Harding was her husband's business partner and an important part of the success of the Marion Star. *Although their marriage had its share of troubles and her husband's administration was marked by scandal, Flossie Harding loved the White House and the role of first lady. The Hardings had no children together.*

Calvin and Grace Coolidge had two sons, one of whom died tragically at the age of sixteen during his father's presidential campaign. Grace Goodhue Coolidge, a Vermont native like her husband, was a lip reading instructor at the Clarke Institute for the Deaf in Northampton, Massachusetts, when she met Coolidge. After his death she continued her work as a teacher of the deaf and, during World War II, became involved in Red Cross relief efforts.

CALVIN COOLIDGE
1872–1933
THIRTIETH PRESIDENT 1923–1929

Born on the fourth of July in 1872 in Plymouth, Vermont, John Calvin Coolidge—known throughout his life by his middle name to avoid confusion with his father—was fifty-one years old when he assumed the presidency upon the death of Warren Harding. A self-reliant New Englander known as "Silent Cal" for his stoicism, Coolidge brought seventeen years of government experience to the presidency.

Like so many American presidents, Calvin Coolidge began his career as a lawyer. He earned a bachelor's degree at Amherst College in central Massachusetts and went on to study law in nearby Northampton. He was admitted to the Massachusetts bar in 1897 and soon thereafter began his own independent practice. Over the next two decades Coolidge worked his way up through the ranks of the Massachusetts Republican party, rising from the Massachusetts General Court to the governor's office.

In 1920 Coolidge won the office of vice president as the running mate of Warren Harding. He became president three years later when Harding died in office and in 1924 won election to his own term. President Coolidge, who believed that thrift was the greatest of all virtues and that too much government was a danger to the people, won public disapproval quickly with his veto of two very popular bills. Coolidge opposed the Veterans Bonus Bill, which promised World War I veterans a paid insurance policy, payable in two decades. This bill passed despite the president's veto. Coolidge also opposed, this time successfully, a farm relief bill aimed at helping farmers by requiring the government to buy surplus crops. Coolidge saw this as undue government interference and twice used his veto to kill the bill. One issue on which Coolidge and the American people were in agreement was the Kellogg-Briand Pact, in which fourteen countries joined the United States in a pledge to resolve all future international conflicts by peaceful means.

In the years of great national prosperity and optimism that followed America's leadership in World War I, Calvin Coolidge was a popular president despite many unpopular decisions. Nonetheless, he did not seek a second term and retired with his wife, Grace, to Northampton. The former president devoted his time to the writing of his autobiography and to a regular newspaper column called "Talking Things Over with Calvin Coolidge." He died in 1933 at his home in Northampton.

One of two presidents to come from Vermont, Calvin Coolidge was born in the small town of Plymouth on the fourth of July in 1872. His father, John Coolidge, was a storekeeper, a farmer, and also a state legislator. Calvin Coolidge lived a classic rural New England childhood, helping with farm chores, collecting maple syrup in the spring, and horseback riding through the countryside.

There is another element, more important than all, without which there cannot be the slightest hope of a permanent peace. That element lies in the heart of humanity. Unless the desire for peace be cherished there, unless this fundamental and only natural source of brotherly love be cultivated to its highest degree, all artificial efforts will be in vain. Peace will come when there is realization that only under a reign of law, based on righteousness and supported by the religious conviction of the brotherhood of man, can there be any hope of a complete and satisfying life. Parchment will fail, the sword will fail, it is only the spiritual nature of man that can be triumphant.

from Calvin Coolidge's Inaugural Address, delivered March 4, 1925

HERBERT HOOVER
1874–1964
THIRTY-FIRST PRESIDENT 1929–1933

The first Quaker president, Iowa native Herbert Hoover was a hard-working, confident man who trained as a mining engineer and first came to the notice of the American people for his relief efforts in Europe during World War I. Hoover was in the White House only eight months before the October, 1929, stock market crash sent the country into the Great Depression.

Born in 1874 in West Branch, Iowa, Hoover attended Quaker schools as a child and later worked at a variety of jobs to support himself through Stanford University in California. At Stanford, Hoover met his future wife, fellow mining major Lou Henry. After their marriage in 1899, the Hoovers lived for a time in China, where Hoover worked as a mining engineer during the Boxer Rebellion. They had two sons, both of whom followed their parents into engineering.

For eighteen years, Hoover worked as a mining engineer, with little thought of a career in politics. He began to change his thinking, however, during the war. As head of efforts to distribute food throughout Europe, Hoover earned a reputation as an efficient and skilled leader. After the war, his efforts were rewarded with an appointment as secretary of commerce. From there he won the presidency, his first ever elective office, in 1928.

Herbert Hoover ran for president on the wave of prosperity sweeping the nation in the decade after World War I. His party's famous pledge of "a chicken in every pot and a car in every garage" reflected a mood of optimism and confidence across America. Hoover won the 1928 election in a landslide victory.

The Great Depression soon crushed the nation's optimism, however, and quickly consumed Hoover's presidency. Hoover, unfortunately, ignored the severity of the nation's economic plight. He held fast to his belief that government should not interfere with business or the economy and resisted cries for federal relief. As unemployment soared and farms failed, Hoover, insisting that the worst was over, became the focus of anger and frustration. Groups of homeless set up cities of cardboard houses they called "Hoovervilles," covering themselves with newspapers they mockingly called "Hoover blankets." More trouble came in the form of fifteen thousand veterans who marched to Washington to demand early payment of the Veterans Bonus promised to them in the Veterans Bonus Bill of the Coolidge administration. Hoover called in federal forces to disperse the angry men, a move that confirmed public opinion of him as a man blind to the nation's suffering.

Herbert Hoover lost his bid for reelection to Franklin Roosevelt. He retired with Lou to California, where he openly opposed the reforms of the Roosevelt administration and remained involved in public life for thirty years. He died in New York City in 1964.

The first president to be born west of the Mississippi River, Herbert Hoover, thanks to his work as a mining engineer, was independently wealthy when he took office, and he donated his presidential salary to charity. Hoover left office an unpopular leader and became a vocal opponent of Roosevelt's New Deal. He returned to public life during the Truman administration, serving on several commissions aimed at cutting waste in government.

And what have been the results of our American system? Our country has become the land of opportunity to those born without inheritance, not merely because of the wealth of its resources and industry, but because of its freedom of initiative and enterprise. Russia has natural resources equal to ours. Her people are equally industrious, but she has not had the lesson of one hundred and fifty years of our form of government and our social system. . . .

The greatness of America has grown out of a political and social system and a method of control of economic forces distinctly its own—our American system—which has carried this great experiment in human welfare further than ever before in all history. We are nearer today to the ideal of abolition of poverty and fear from the lives of men and women than ever before in any land. And I again repeat that the departure from our American system by injecting principles destructive to it which our opponents propose will jeopardize the very liberty and freedom of our people, will destroy equality of opportunity, not alone to ourselves, but to our children.

from a campaign speech by Herbert Hoover, 1928

FRANKLIN DELANO ROOSEVELT
1882–1945
THIRTY-SECOND PRESIDENT 1933–1945

Four times Americans went to the polls and elected Franklin Delano Roosevelt as their president. An inspirational and controversial leader, Roosevelt steered Americans through the dark, troubled days of the Great Depression and World War II.

Franklin Roosevelt grew up in the luxurious family home in Hyde Park, New York, and spent summers on beautiful Campobello Island. Despite his rather narrow experience of wealth and privilege, as president, Roosevelt became known as the champion of the poor and downtrodden. With the country in the throes of the Great Depression, FDR, a Harvard graduate and former assistant secretary of the navy and governor of New York, ran for president on the promise of a "New Deal," a package of programs aimed at providing economic relief to a country in crisis. In his twelve years as president, Roosevelt oversaw an unprecedented expansion of the federal government. The New Deal included programs to create jobs for the unemployed, to regulate banking and housing, to extend electric power to rural areas, and to stimulate business; he also began Social Security, the government program to provide income to the elderly and the disabled. Under Roosevelt, as never before, the federal government took on the responsibility of providing for those Americans who could not provide for themselves. His administration was not without controversy, and his programs were not universally embraced; but Franklin Roosevelt rose to the occasion at a time of great crisis in America and left an indelible mark on U.S. history. Despite his own failing health, Roosevelt projected an image of strength and vitality and brought comfort and hope to countless American families.

Roosevelt's wife, Eleanor, a niece of former president Theodore Roosevelt and a distant cousin to Franklin, was, like her husband, a popular and controversial figure. She was an outspoken advocate of civil and human rights and as first lady took an active role in American public life. After her husband's death, Mrs. Roosevelt continued her activism, serving for a time as delegate to the United Nations, where she chaired the Commission on Human Rights. Eleanor and Franklin Roosevelt had five children.

Stricken with polio at age thirty-nine, and thereafter confined to a wheel chair, Franklin Roosevelt defied his physical limitations for three terms in the White House. At the start of his fourth term, however, his health began to deteriorate. He died in office in 1945, only months before the end of World War II.

Serious and shy as a young woman, Eleanor Roosevelt was a twenty-year-old social worker in New York when she married her distant cousin Franklin in 1905. In 1921, however, when Franklin was stricken by polio, Eleanor found the confidence and strength to fight against her mother-in-law's wishes that Franklin retire from public life and urged him to remain active. With Eleanor's help and guidance Franklin did continue on, all the way to the White House. As first lady, Eleanor Roosevelt was an entirely new breed. She took her obligation to help the nation's less fortunate as a sacred duty and could be found anywhere from a soup kitchen to an inner city neighborhood to a civil rights protest. Eleanor Roosevelt expanded the role of the first lady and opened American eyes to the real power and possibilities of women in the public arena.

I see a great nation, upon a great continent, blessed with a great wealth of natural resources. Its hundred and thirty million people are at peace among themselves; they are making their country a good neighbor among nations. I see a United States which can demonstrate that, under democratic methods of government, national wealth can be translated into a spreading volume of human comforts hitherto unknown, and the lowest standard of living can be raised far above the level of mere subsistence.

But here is the challenge to our democracy: In this nation I see tens of millions of its citizens—a substantial part of its whole population—who at this very moment are denied the greater part of what the very lowest standards of today call the necessities of life.

I see millions of families trying to live on incomes so meager that the pall of family disaster hangs over them day by day.

I see millions whose daily lives in the city and on the farm continue under conditions labeled indecent by so-called polite society half a century ago.

I see millions denied education, recreation, and the opportunity to better their lot and the lot of their children.

I see millions lacking the means to buy products of farm and factory and by their poverty denying work and productiveness to many other millions.

I see one-third a nation ill-housed, ill-clad, ill-nourished.

It is not in despair that I paint you that picture. I paint it for you in hope—because the nation, seeing and understanding the injustice in it, proposes to paint it out. We are determined to make every American citizen the subject of his country's interest and concern; and we will never regard any faithful, law-abiding group within our borders as superfluous.

The test of our progress is not whether we add more to the abundance of those who have much; it is whether we provide enough for those who had too little.

If I know aught of the spirit and purpose of our Nation, we will not listen to Comfort, Opportunism, and Timidity. We will carry on. . . .

Today, we reconsecrate our country to long cherished ideals in a suddenly changed civilization. In every land there are always at work forces that drive men apart and forces that draw men together. In our personal ambitions we are individualists. But in our seeking for economic and political progress as a nation, we all go up, or else we all go down, as one people.

from Franklin Delano Roosevelt's second Inaugural Address,
delivered January 20, 1937

HARRY S TRUMAN
1884–1972
THIRTY-THIRD PRESIDENT 1945–1953

Humble, plainspoken Harry S Truman was the son of a Missouri farm family who won the hearts of the American people with his no-nonsense, honest leadership. A high school graduate without the money to attend college, Truman tried unsuccessfully to make a start in business and spent a decade running the family farm before service in World War I revealed his skills as a leader and led him into a lifetime of public service.

Born at the family home in Lamar, Missouri, in 1884, Truman grew up in and around Independence, moving back and forth from farm to town following his father's latest venture. He was a slight child who wore glasses to correct extreme nearsightedness. It was as a child in Independence that Harry met his future wife, Elizabeth "Bess" Wallace.

Truman was running the family farm in Grandview, Missouri, when World War I began. He volunteered and served nearly two years, rising from lieutenant to major and discovering along the way that he had a knack for leadership. He returned to Missouri in 1919 with new connections and new ambitions. After one failed business venture, Truman won election as judge of Jackson County, Missouri. He remained in that post for twelve years, earning a reputation as an honest, hard-working, successful public servant. In 1934 Truman ran for Senate and, with the backing of powerful Missouri Democrats, won the election. After a decade of Senate membership, Truman was called upon by President Roosevelt to be his running mate in the 1944 election. Truman, at first hesitant, accepted the vice presidential nomination, and the two went on to victory. He served as vice president less than three months before Roosevelt's death elevated him to the highest office in the land.

Harry Truman's most difficult decision came within his first six months as president. In August of 1945 President Truman ordered atomic bombs dropped on Hiroshima and Nagasaki, Japan. He made the decision aware of the likely devastation but believing that the bombs would end the war and save American soldiers inestimable suffering and death. His decision led to the end of World War II, and the United States emerged as a world leader with great power and great responsibilities. President Truman then faced the difficult challenge of leading America into the Cold War era. Responding to the threat of Soviet aggression in Europe, Truman declared it U.S. policy to support people around the world in their fight against communism. He led the United States into the United Nations and with Secretary of State George Marshall devised the Marshall Plan for rebuilding Europe after the devastation of the war. In 1948 Truman won the confidence of the people and defied political odds to win election as president in his own right.

Harry Truman left office after two terms and returned to Independence with Bess, where he lived until his death.

Pictured below is the Wallace family home in Independence, Missouri, where Harry Truman lived after his marriage to Bess and to which they returned by train at the end of his presidential term. Truman, as unassuming as this house, carried the "S" in his name without a period; his parents gave their son "S" in lieu of a middle name to honor his paternal grandfather, Anderson Shippe Truman, and his maternal grandfather, Solomon Young.

Each period of our national history has had its special challenges. Those that confront us now are as momentous as any in the past. Today marks the beginning not only of a new administration, but of a period that will be eventful, perhaps decisive, for us and for the world.

It may be our lot to experience, and in large measure to bring about, a major turning point in the long history of the human race. The first half of this century has been marked by unprecedented and brutal attacks on the rights of man, and by the two most frightful wars in history. The supreme need of our time is for men to learn to live together in peace and harmony.

The peoples of the earth face the future with grave uncertainty, composed almost equally of great hopes and great fears. In this time of doubt, they look to the United States as never before for good will, strength, and wise leadership.

It is fitting, therefore, that we take this occasion to proclaim to the world the essential principles of the faith by which we live, and to declare our aims to all peoples.

The American people stand firm in the faith which has inspired this nation from the beginning. We believe that all men have a right to equal justice under law and equal opportunity to share in the common good. We believe that all men have the right to freedom of thought and expression. We believe that all men are created equal because they are created in the image of God.

From this faith we will not be moved.

The American people desire, and are determined to work for, a world in which all nations and all peoples are free to govern themselves as they see fit and to achieve a decent and satisfying life. Above all else, our people desire, and are determined to work for, peace on earth— a just and lasting peace— based on genuine agreement freely arrived at by equals.

*from Harry S Truman's
Inaugural Address,
delivered January 20, 1949*

One of the most famous political photographs of all time captures the excitement of Harry S Truman's unexpected victory over Thomas Dewey in the 1948 presidential election. Truman, considered an underdog by political observers who saw him only as the man who had filled in for Roosevelt, took matters into his own hands with a 30,000-mile "whistlestop" campaign trip. Truman's tough, direct manner of speaking and his common Missouri farm roots appealed to the American people, who cheered their president with cries of "Give'em Hell, Harry!" and stood behind him on election day.

DWIGHT D. EISENHOWER
1890–1969
THIRTY-FOURTH PRESIDENT 1953–1961

Born in Texas and raised in Abilene, Kansas, David Dwight Eisenhower grew up in a poor family, one of seven boys. Known as Dwight David to avoid confusion with his father and nicknamed "Ike" from childhood, Eisenhower loved sports and military history. He enrolled at West Point at the age of twenty-one and from then on made the United States military his career. He held only one elected office in his life, that of president of the United States.

At West Point, Eisenhower showed no signs of the great military leader he would one day become. Young Eisenhower was interested in one thing: sports, in particular football. Eisenhower even considered leaving the Academy during his second year after a football injury put a permanent end to his playing career. He stayed on as a coach, however, and graduated in 1915 with the rank of second lieutenant. For all but two of the next thirty-seven years, Eisenhower served in the United States Army. It was during World War II that Eisenhower rose to prominence, becoming Supreme Allied Commander and, after the successful Allied landing at Normandy, a five-star general. In 1950 President Truman appointed Eisenhower supreme commander of NATO, a position he held until his nomination for president in July of 1952.

With Senator Richard M. Nixon as his running mate, Dwight Eisenhower won the 1952 presidential election based in great part on his war record and his strong, no-nonsense personality. Popular in office as he had been as a candidate, Eisenhower won reelection in a second landslide four years later. In office, Eisenhower immediately lived up to his campaign promise and traveled to Korea to speed up the negotiations that ended the war. His administration was characterized by what is known as the Eisenhower Doctrine, a bold statement of the American stand against communism. A deeply religious man who made prayer a part of his daily White House routine, Eisenhower believed that strength was necessary not for its own sake, but for its power as a deterrent to war, and he began to build up the American nuclear arsenal. Eisenhower felt strongly that the United States had the right and obligation to protect any country threatened by the spread of communism.

Eisenhower, a kind and good-hearted man who never spoke ill of his opponents and never lost the goodwill of the American people, retired from public life in 1961 after attending the inauguration of his successor, John F. Kennedy. He and his wife, Mamie, then moved to Gettysburg, Pennsylvania, their first permanent home in almost forty-five years of married life. Eisenhower died nine years later after a series of heart attacks. He was buried in his army uniform in Abilene, Kansas.

Dwight Eisenhower and Mamie Doud married in 1916. In more than fifty years of married life, the Eisenhowers moved twenty-eight times throughout the United States, Panama, and the Philippines. They had one son.

Down the long lane of the history yet to be written America knows that this world of ours, ever growing smaller, must avoid becoming a community of dreadful fear and hate, and be, instead, a proud confederation of mutual trust and respect.

Such a confederation must be one of equals. The weakest must come to the conference table with the same confidence as we do, protected as we are by our moral, economic, and military strength. That table, though scarred by many past frustrations, cannot be abandoned for the certain agony of the battlefield.

Disarmament, with mutual honor and confidence, is a continuing imperative. Together we must learn how to compose differences, not with arms, but with intellect and decent purpose. Because this need is so sharp and apparent, I confess that I lay down my official responsibilities in this field with a definite sense of disappointment. As one who has witnessed the horror and lingering sadness of war—as one who knows that another war could utterly destroy this civilization which has been so slowly and painfully built over thousands of years—I wish I could say tonight that a lasting peace is in sight.*

Happily, I can say that war has been avoided. Steady progress toward our ultimate goal has been made. But, so much remains to be done. As a private citizen, I shall never cease to do what little I can to help the world advance along that road. . . .

from Dwight Eisenhower's Farewell Address, delivered on January 17, 1961, three days before the inauguration of John F. Kennedy

Dwight Eisenhower was a brigadier general when World War II began. After the attack on Pearl Harbor, President Roosevelt called Eisenhower to Washington and appointed him assistant chief of staff in charge of war plans. By 1942 he was Allied Commander-in-Chief, overseeing the battles in North Africa and Italy. Roosevelt promoted Eisenhower to Supreme Allied Commander in December of 1943, and it was in this capacity that he planned the D-Day landing at Normandy. Eisenhower was a five-star general when he accepted the surrender of Germany at Rheims on May 7, 1945.

John Fitzgerald Kennedy married Jacqueline Bouvier on September 12, 1953, in Newport, Rhode Island. When her husband was elected president, Jackie became one of the most popular of first ladies, bringing a new style and energy to the White House. She invited musicians and artists to the White House and redecorated much of the historic home with original furnishings. After the president's death, Jackie Kennedy took great care to see that their two young children grew up away from the public eye.

JOHN F. KENNEDY
1917–1963
THIRTY-FIFTH PRESIDENT 1961–1963

The youngest man ever elected president, and the first Roman Catholic, forty-three-year-old John Fitzgerald Kennedy won the White House with his pledge to lead America to meet the challenge and the promise of the future. Young, handsome, and charismatic, John Kennedy won a close race against Richard M. Nixon but would be denied by an assassin's bullet the chance to complete his term.

The son of Joseph Kennedy, a prominent, wealthy Massachusetts businessman and diplomat, and Rose Fitzgerald Kennedy, whose father was mayor of Boston, John Kennedy was born in Brookline, Massachusetts, in 1917 and lived a childhood of great privilege. A fun-loving, active youth despite frequent illnesses, Kennedy did not take his education seriously until his junior year at Harvard, when he began to think of a future in politics. After graduation, Kennedy served in the navy, where his heroism after the bombing of his boat, the *PT-109,* won him the Purple Heart and national recognition.

After the war, Kennedy worked briefly as a journalist before beginning his career in politics with a successful run for the United States House as a Democratic representative from Massachusetts. From the House, Kennedy went on to the Senate, where he served for eight years before making his successful run for the presidency. In his race against Republican Richard Nixon, Kennedy was helped immeasurably by the advent of extensive television coverage, which gave the advantage to the more attractive, more charismatic Kennedy.

In his three years in office, John Kennedy, along with his wife, Jacqueline Bouvier Kennedy, and their two young children, captured the imagination of the American people and brought new life to Washington, D.C. Admired as much for his style as for his skills as a leader, Kennedy enjoyed great popularity. He inherited a nation near crisis with the Soviet Union and continued to struggle with the threat of communism that had troubled former president Eisenhower. During the Kennedy years, U.S. involvement in the Vietnam conflict grew quickly. The Berlin Wall went up, and tensions with the Soviets rose to near crisis during the standoff over Soviet missile installations in Cuba. Kennedy is remembered for his strong stand against spreading communism and most beloved for his innovations in the Peace Corps, the space program, and his stand on Civil Rights.

John F. Kennedy was assassinated on November 22, 1963, in Dallas, Texas, in what has proven to be one of the most studied and controversial crimes in American history. Lee Harvey Oswald, a former marine with Marxist sympathies, was arrested for the shooting but was himself shot and killed before he could be tried.

John Kennedy called his program for change in America "The New Frontier." One innovative program was the Peace Corps, established in March of 1961. The Peace Corps was created to organize, train, and place American volunteers in underdeveloped nations across the world. Volunteers would serve for at least two years as teachers, health care workers, and technical advisors in local communities. In the first twenty years of the Corps, more than 85,000 Americans volunteered and served.

In the long history of the world, only a few generations have been granted the role of defending freedom in its hour of maximum danger. I do not shrink from this responsibility— I welcome it. I do not believe that any of us would exchange places with any other people or any other generation. The energy, the faith, the devotion which we bring to this endeavor will light our country and all who serve it— and the glow from that fire can truly light the world.

And so my fellow Americans, ask not what your country can do for you—ask what you can do for your country.

My fellow citizens of the world: ask not what America will do for you, but what together we can do for the freedom of man.

Finally, whether you are citizens of America or citizens of the world, ask of us here the same high standards of strength and sacrifice which we ask of you. With a good conscience our only sure reward, with history the final judge of our deeds, let us go forth to lead the land we love, asking His blessing and His help, but knowing that here on earth God's work must truly be our own.

from John F. Kennedy's Inaugural Address, delivered January 20, 1961

LYNDON B. JOHNSON
1908–1973
THIRTY-SIXTH PRESIDENT 1963–1969

Lyndon Baines Johnson took the oath of office aboard the presidential aircraft Air Force One on a runway at Dallas's Love Field airport just hours after the assassination of President John F. Kennedy. A big, strong man with roots in Texas and more than a quarter century's worth of experience in public office, Johnson assumed the presidency amid great turmoil and served during one of the most tumultuous periods in American history.

Born in the family farmhouse on the Pedernales River near Johnson City, Texas, Lyndon Johnson grew up on Texas legends and Texas politics. His father, a farmer and a state legislator, was an early role model for his son. Johnson worked himself through college and taught high school briefly before beginning his own career in public service. Johnson's first job was as secretary to a Democratic representative from Texas. Soon thereafter he himself won election to the House. For the next twenty-two years Lyndon Johnson represented Texas in the House and then the Senate, rising to become Senate majority leader in 1955—at forty-six the youngest man ever to hold that position—and earning a reputation as a persuasive and powerful legislator. Johnson's great influence in Washington and his popularity in Texas convinced John Kennedy to choose him as his running mate in 1960.

After completing John Kennedy's unfinished term, Johnson won reelection in his own right. In all he served as president for five years. His greatest burden was the Vietnam conflict. Although there was no official declaration of war, American involvement in the conflict increased during the Johnson administration. President Johnson, though saddened by the number of Americans killed in Vietnam and frustrated by the increasingly violent protest movement at home, was unable to put an end to the conflict or to complete the withdrawal of American forces.

President Johnson's greatest achievements came in the area of civil rights. With his strong support some of the most important civil rights legislation in American history was passed, including the Civil Rights Act of 1964, which outlawed racial discrimination in public facilities; the Voting Rights Act of 1965, which banned literacy tests as a qualification for voter registration; and the Civil Rights Act of 1968, which put an end to racial discrimination in housing.

Worn down by the strains of the presidency, Lyndon Johnson surprised Americans by announcing that he would neither seek nor accept a second complete term. He retired in January of 1969 to his LBJ Ranch in Texas, where he died in January of 1973. At his funeral, the Reverend Billy Graham spoke; and Johnson's favorite hymn, "The Battle Hymn of the Republic," was sung. He was survived by his wife, Claudia "Lady Bird" Johnson, and their two daughters, Lynda Bird and Luci Baines Johnson.

Lyndon Johnson had great ambitions for public life: "I want to be the president who educated young children to the wonders of their world . . .who helped feed the hungry . . .who helped the poor to find their own way and who protected the right of every citizen to vote in every election." Although he struggled with the conflict in Vietnam and civil unrest at home, Johnson did win praise from many for his "war on poverty," which included Medicare and Medicaid, and for the significant progress made during his administration in American civil rights. Johnson's wife, Lady Bird, devoted her energies as first lady to preserving and beautifying the American landscape. She traveled across the country to promote the Highway Beautification Act of 1965, which controlled the placement of billboards along national highways. In recognition of her work, a section of Redwood National Park was named the Lady Bird Johnson Grove.

The time has come for Americans of all races and creeds and political beliefs to understand and respect one another.

Let us put an end to the teaching and preaching of hate and evil and violence. Let us turn away from the fanatics of the far left and the far right, from the apostles of bitterness and bigotry, from those defiant of law, and those who pour venom into our nation's bloodstream. . . .

These are the United States—a united people with unity of purpose.

Our American unity does not depend upon unanimity. We have differences; but now, as in the past, we can derive from those differences strength, not weakness, wisdom, not despair. Both as a people and as a government we can unite upon a program which is wise and just, enlightened and constructive.

from Lyndon B. Johnson's Address to Congress, November 27, 1963

RICHARD M. NIXON
1913–1994
THIRTY-SEVENTH PRESIDENT 1969–1974

Born in 1913 in Yorba Linda, California, Richard Milhous Nixon, a Quaker, grew up in poverty. A serious and ambitious child from the start, Nixon rose each morning before dawn to work in his family's grocery store before school and was known as "Gloomy Gus" for his rigid demeanor. Nixon did well in local public schools and at Whittier College before heading east for Duke Law School, where he graduated with honors and was elected president of his class. After law school, Nixon returned to California and joined a Whittier law firm. World War II interrupted his law career, and after four years in the navy, he once again returned to California, this time with political ambitions.

In 1947 Nixon won a seat in the House of Representatives, where he gained national recognition for his work on the House Un-American Activities Committee. His notoriety helped him win a seat in the Senate in 1950; two years later, Nixon was the Republican party's choice as running mate for presidential candidate Dwight Eisenhower. Swept into office, thanks in large part to Eisenhower's great popularity, Nixon served eight years as vice president before making his own failed bid for the White House in 1960.

Narrowly beaten, Nixon returned once more to California after John Kennedy took office. After a failed run for governor, he retired from public life for six years. But his ambition was not to be denied. In 1968, with the country torn apart by the conflict in Vietnam, Nixon finally won the presidency with a promise to bring back law and order to a country in turmoil.

The Nixon administration had two great international successes. In 1972 Nixon journeyed to China where he met with Chairman Mao Tse-tung, breaking the silence between the two nations. Nixon was the first president to visit China. In the historic meeting, the two leaders agreed to increase trade and cultural contacts between China and the United States. Nixon also began the Strategic Arms Limitations Talks with the Soviet Union, signing the first SALT Treaty along with Soviet leader Leonid Brezhnev. Nixon also oversaw final American withdrawal from Vietnam in 1973.

Nixon won reelection in 1972 but within months was embroiled in one of the worst political scandals in American history. In June of 1972, members of the

Committee to Reelect the President were arrested for a break-in at Democratic National Headquarters in the Washington office building known as Watergate. Over the next two years, news reporters discovered that the break-in was part of a larger Republican plot to sabotage Democrat opponents and that President Nixon himself played a role in that plot and in the cover-up that followed. Maintaining his innocence, Nixon resigned on August 9, 1974, to avoid impeachment.

Nixon was pardoned of all criminal wrongdoing by Gerald Ford in September of 1974. He and his wife, Pat, retired to San Clemente, California. Married since 1940, the Nixons had met when they were cast opposite each other in an amateur theater production in Whittier. An ambitious and smitten Nixon proposed the night of their very first meeting, but Pat did not accept until two years later. The Nixons had two daughters.

In the years after leaving office, Richard Nixon regained the respect of many Americans in government and used his knowledge of international relations to serve as an unofficial American ambassador, traveling to nearly twenty foreign countries and meeting with many heads of state.

Richard Nixon died on April 22, 1994, in New York City. He is buried on the grounds of the Nixon Presidential Library and Museum in Yorba Linda, California.

In February of 1972 President Richard M. Nixon set out on a trip to Communist China that he called "a journey for peace." It was a bold and controversial overture at a time when anti-communist sentiments were running high in America. In China, Nixon met with Chairman Mao Tse-tung and Premier Chou En-lai. The three leaders agreed to broaden the scope of relations between the two nations despite the fact that official diplomatic ties did not exist. At home, Nixon was hailed for his diplomatic skill.

Each moment in history is a fleeting time, precious and unique. But some stand out as moments of beginning, in which courses are set that shape decades or centuries.

This can be such a moment.

Forces are now converging that make possible, for the first time, the hope that many of man's deepest aspirations can at last be realized.

The spiraling pace of change allows us to contemplate, within our own lifetime, advances that once would have taken centuries.

In throwing wide the horizons of space, we have discovered new horizons on earth.

For the first time, because the people of the world want peace and the leaders of the world are afraid of war, the times are on the side of peace.

Eight years from now America will celebrate its 200th anniversary as a nation. Within the lifetime of most people now living, mankind will celebrate that great new year which comes only once in a thousand years—the beginning of the Third Millennium.

What kind of nation will we be, what kind of world will we live in, whether we shape the future in the image of our hopes, is ours to determine by our actions and our choices.

The greatest honor history can bestow is the title of peacemaker. This honor now beckons America—the chance to help lead the world at last out of the valley of turmoil, and onto that high ground of peace that man has dreamed of since the dawn of civilization.

If we succeed, generations to come will say of us now living that we mastered our moment, that we helped make the world safe for mankind.

This is our summons to greatness.

I believe the American people are ready to answer this call.

*from Richard M. Nixon's first Inaugural Address,
delivered January 20, 1969*

GERALD R. FORD
1913–2006
THIRTY-EIGHTH PRESIDENT 1974–1977

Gerald Rudolph Ford had been a member of the House of Representatives for nearly twenty-five years and was planning to retire after one more term when an unprecedented series of events elevated him to the office of vice president and then that of president within a ten-month period. Ford, a native of Grand Rapids, Michigan, and House minority leader, became vice president following the resignation of Spiro Agnew in October of 1973. The following August, he acceded to the presidency to replace Richard Nixon, who had resigned during the Watergate scandal.

Gerald Ford was born Leslie Lynch King, Jr., in Omaha, Nebraska, in 1913. His name was legally changed in 1916 when his mother remarried. Ford always considered his stepfather, Gerald R. Ford, Sr., to be his true father. Ford spent his childhood in Grand Rapids, Michigan, where he was a hard-working, popular, and athletic youth. From 1949 to 1973, Ford, an honest and unpretentious man, represented the state of Michigan in Washington. A navy veteran and college football star who had passed up the chance at a career in professional football to attend Yale Law School, Ford was a committed public servant who had never had presidential ambitions. Married since 1948 to his wife Betty, Ford was father to four children. In his youth he had been a star athlete and an Eagle Scout. He was chosen by Nixon to replace Agnew because of his moderate Republican rep-

utation in the House and his clean-cut, wholesome image with the American people.

In the White House, Ford immediately pardoned Richard Nixon for all connections to the Watergate break-in and the subsequent cover-up. During his three year term he struggled against inflation, a recession, and the lingering distrust of the American people still shocked by the misdeeds of the Nixon years. Ford sought a second term but lost to Jimmy Carter. He retired to California and a life of writing, speaking, and recreation with his wife, Betty.

Gerald Ford passed away on December 26, 2006. After ceremonies in California, Washington D.C., and Grand Rapids, Michigan, he was buried on the grounds of the Gerald R. Ford Museum in Grand Rapids.

Gerald Ford served in the navy for four years during and after World War II. He began as a physical fitness instructor but in 1943 requested sea duty and was assigned to the USS Monterey *in the South Pacific. Ford served as a gunnery officer and later as assistant navigator and earned ten battle stars on board the* Monterey *during battles at Wake Island, Okinawa, and the Philippines. After the war, Ford returned to his legal practice in Grand Rapids, Michigan.*

To the peoples and governments of all friendly nations, and I hope that encompasses the whole world, I pledge an uninterrupted and sincere search for peace. America will remain strong and united, but its strength will remain dedicated to the safety and sanity of the entire family of man, as well as to our own precious freedom. I believe that truth is the glue that holds the government together, not only our government but civilization itself. That bond though strained, is unbroken at home and abroad. In all my public and private acts as your President, I expect to follow my instincts of openness and candor with full confidence that honesty is always the best policy in the end.

My fellow Americans, our long national nightmare is over.

Our Constitution works; our great Republic is a government of laws and not of men. Here the people rule. But there is a higher power, by whatever name we honor him, who ordains not only righteousness but love, not only justice, but mercy. . . .

With all the strength and all the good sense I have gained from life, with all the confidence my family, my friends, and my dedicated staff impart me, and with the good will of countless Americans I have encountered in recent visits to forty states, I now solemnly reaffirm my promise I made to you . . . to uphold the Constitution, to do what is right as God gives me to see the right, and to do the very best I can for America.

God helping me, I will not let you down.

Gerald Ford, speaking in 1974

Gerald Ford, pictured here at the White House with Japanese Emperor Hirohito and his wife, did not seek the presidency, but he served with the same loyalty that he had displayed in nearly a quarter century of public service. His wife, Betty, had been looking forward to retirement in Grand Rapids. Instead, she found herself in the very visible role of first lady. In the White House, Mrs. Ford was an advocate of the Equal Rights Amendment. She also did much work for the mentally retarded. Her greatest contribution to American life, however, was her openness following her fight against breast cancer. Mrs. Ford was an inspiration to many women who had suffered similarly, and her willingness to discuss her illness led to increased awareness of the disease and its prevention.

JIMMY CARTER
1924–
THIRTY-NINTH PRESIDENT
1977–1981

began in 1963 after he won a seat in the Georgia State Senate. His success there led to a run for governor in 1970. As governor, Carter gained prominence as a leader of the "New South" as he fought to improve education and put an end to segregation and discrimination. In 1976 Carter won the Democratic nomination and defeated incumbent Gerald Ford to win the presidency.

From the beginning of his term, Carter sought to reduce the "pomp and circumstance" of the presidency by, among other things, walking to the White House after his inauguration, rather than riding in a limousine, and halting the playing of "Hail to the Chief" during public appearances. Carter was an outspoken proponent of international human rights, condemning Soviet aggression in Afghanistan and joining with sixty-three other nations in a boycott of the Olympic Games in Moscow. Carter was also instrumental in the Camp David Accords of 1978 between Israel and Egypt, which led to the end of a thirty-one-year-old war between the two nations. The darkest hour of the Carter years, however—and the one for which he may always be remembered—was the taking of more than sixty American hostages at the United States embassy in Tehran, Iran, on November 4, 1979. Fifty-two American hostages remained in captivity four hundred and forty-four days. Carter's attempts at gaining their freedom were unsuccessful. The hostages were not released from Iran until January 20, 1981, the very day that Carter left office.

Jimmy Carter lost his bid for reelection in 1980 and retired to Georgia. Although he left office an unpopular president, Carter has since become one of our most visible and beloved former leaders. His Carter Presidential Center in Atlanta works to promote human rights; and he and Rosalynn, with whom he has three sons and one daughter, are active members of the group Habitat for Humanity, which builds houses for low-income families.

James Earl Carter, Jr., a Georgia peanut farmer who even as president signed his name "Jimmy," was born in 1924 in Plains, Georgia, the first president to be born in a hospital. An introspective, disciplined man with an informal manner and a soft southern drawl, Carter learned his early lessons from his father, James Earl, Sr., a farmer and state legislator, and his mother, Lillian, a nurse and outspoken civil rights advocate. Carter and his wife, Rosalynn, were both devout Baptists who made prayer and Bible reading a part of their daily White House routine.

Carter grew up on his father's farm and attended local public schools in and around Plains. Inspired by an uncle who was a navy radioman, he accepted an appointment to the Naval Academy in 1943 and planned on a career in the military. When his father died in 1953, however, Jimmy returned to Georgia to run the family peanut farm. His career in public service

I have just taken the oath of office on the Bible my mother gave me just a few years ago, opened to a timeless admonition from the ancient prophet Micah: "He hath showed thee, O man, what is good; and what doth the Lord require of thee, but to do justly, and to love mercy, and to walk humbly with thy God. . . ." The American dream endures. We must once again have faith in our country—and in one another. . . . Let our recent mistakes bring a resurgent commitment to the basic principles of our nation, for we know that if we despise our own government we have no future. . . . Our commitment to human rights must be absolute, our laws fair, our national beauty preserved; the powerful must not persecute the weak, and human dignity must be enhanced. . . . We pledge perseverance and wisdom in our efforts to limit the world's armaments to those necessary to each nation's own domestic safety. We will move this year a step toward our ultimate goal—the elimination of all nuclear weapons from this earth.

We urge all people to join us, for success can mean life instead of death.

Our nation can be strong abroad only if it is strong at home, and we know that the best way to enhance freedom in other lands is to demonstrate here that our democratic system is worthy of emulation. . . .

The passion for freedom is on the rise . . . we will maintain strength so sufficient that it need not be proven in combat—a quiet strength based not merely on the size of the arsenal but on the nobility of the ideas . . . we will fight our wars against poverty, ignorance, and injustice, for those are the enemies against which our forces can be honorably marshaled.

We are a proudly idealistic nation, but let no one confuse our idealism with weakness. . . . When my time as your president has ended . . . I would hope that the nations of the world might say that we had built a lasting peace, based not on weapons of war but on international policies which reflect our own most precious values.

from Jimmy Carter's Inaugural Address, delivered January 20, 1977

RONALD REAGAN
1911–2004
FORTIETH PRESIDENT 1981–1989

Known as the "Great Communicator" for the skill with which he used radio and television to speak to the American people, Ronald Reagan defeated Jimmy Carter in the 1980 presidential election with one of the largest electoral landslides in American history. In his two terms in the White House—as the recession ended, unemployment dropped, and relations with the Soviet Union began to thaw—Reagan maintained his unusual hold on the affections of the American people. His strong leadership brought a renewed sense of pride and patriotism to Americans at home and a renewed respect for America throughout the world.

Ronald Wilson Reagan was born in 1911 in Tampico, Illinois. His childhood was spent for the most part in nearby Dixon. After attending local public schools, Reagan went on to Eureka College, where he discovered his love of acting. Upon graduation, Reagan worked briefly as a radio announcer before beginning a thirty-year career as a Hollywood movie actor.

Throughout his acting career Reagan maintained an interest in politics and was often urged by friends to run for office. He was a leader in the Screen Actors Guild for many years and, after voting as a Democrat in his youth, campaigned actively for Republicans Richard Nixon and Barry Goldwater. It was a successful televised campaign speech Reagan delivered for Goldwater in 1964 that convinced him and his supporters that he could win the governor's office in California. In 1967 Ronald Reagan became governor of California and, in two terms, gained national prominence as a strong conservative leader.

In 1976 Reagan mounted an unsuccessful challenge to incumbent Republican Gerald Ford for the party's presidential nomination. Four years later, Reagan ran again against President Jimmy Carter, who was crippled by the deepening recession and his inability to gain the release of the hostages in Iran. Winning 489 electoral votes to Carter's 49, Reagan took office in January of 1981.

At nearly seventy years of age, Ronald Reagan was the oldest man ever to begin a presidency. Yet his

rugged good looks belied his age, and his charm and skill at speaking inspired the confidence of the American people. On Reagan's inauguration day, the American hostages were freed in Iran after more than a year in captivity, and his administration was not much more than a year old when the economy began to expand, lifting the recession and bringing jobs to the unemployed. Reagan won public approval for his firm stance against the Soviet Union. He oversaw the build-up of American defenses to match Soviet strength, and when Mikhail Gorbachev came to power, Reagan moved to improve relations, meeting Gorbachev in famous Iceland summits. At home and abroad, Reagan was seen as a strong, skilled leader, equal to America's position as a world superpower.

After eight years in office, Reagan left the White House in 1989 as one of the most popular presidents in recent history. He and his wife, Nancy, retired to California, where he resided until his death on June 5, 2004.

Ronald Reagan married Nancy Davis in 1952. They met three years earlier when he was the president of the Screen Actors Guild and she, an actress, came to him for help. As first lady, Nancy Reagan was both popular and controversial. She earned disapproval for her lavish spending on decorating and entertaining at a time when her husband was urging all facets of government to cut spending, but she won praise from many for her campaign against drug use among young Americans. Mrs. Reagan exerted a powerful influence on her husband and was fiercely protective of him.

What I am describing now is a plan and a hope for the long term—the march of freedom and democracy which will leave Marxism-Leninism on the ash heap of history as it has left other tyrannies which stifle the freedom and muzzle the self-expression of the people. . . . Our military strength is a prerequisite to peace, but let it be clear we maintain this strength in the hope that it will never be used, for the ultimate determinant in the struggle that's now going on in the world will not be bombs and rockets but a test of wills and ideas, a trial of spiritual resolve, the values we hold, the beliefs we cherish, the ideals to which we are dedicated. . . .

I have often wondered about the shyness of some of us in the West about standing for these ideals that have done so much to ease the plight of man and the hardships of our imperfect world. This reluctance to use those vast resources at our command reminds me of the elderly lady whose home was bombed in the blitz. As the rescuers moved about, they found a bottle of brandy she'd stored behind the staircase, which was all that was left standing. And since she was barely conscious, one of the workers pulled the cork to give her a taste of it. She came around immediately and said, "Here now—there now, put it back. That's for emergencies."

Well, the emergency is upon us. Let us be shy no longer. Let us go to our strength. Let us offer hope. Let us tell the world that a new age is not only possible but probable.

During the dark days of the Second World War, when [England] was incandescent with courage, Winston Churchill exclaimed about Britain's adversaries, "What kind of people do they think we are?" Well, Britain's adversaries found out what extraordinary people the British are. But all the democracies paid a terrible price for allowing the dictators to underestimate us. We dare not make that mistake again. So, let us ask ourselves, "What kind of people do we think we are?" And let us answer, "Free people, worthy of freedom and determined not only to remain so but to help others gain their freedom as well."

from a speech by Ronald Reagan to British Parliament, June 8, 1982

GEORGE H. W. BUSH
1924–
FORTY-FIRST PRESIDENT 1989–1993

After serving loyally as vice president under Ronald Reagan for eight years, George Herbert Walker Bush won the presidency in his own right in 1988. In one of the roughest campaigns in American history, Bush shook off his reputation for weakness and came from behind to soundly defeat Democrat Michael Dukakis. In the four years that followed, Bush proved himself a strong leader in a tumultuous international arena.

George Bush was born to wealth and privilege in 1924 in Milton, Massachusetts. Soon thereafter the family moved to Greenwich, Connecticut. Bush attended prestigious Phillips Academy in Andover, Massachusetts, and was then accepted at Yale University but decided to put off college to enlist in the navy during World War II.

George Bush flew fifty-eight navy combat missions between 1943 and 1945, one of which ended in near disaster when his plane went down off the Bonin Islands. Two members of his crew were killed, and Bush himself came dangerously close to capture by hostile Japanese forces. He was rescued after more than three hours in the Pacific and was awarded the Distinguished Flying Cross. Shortly after his return from the war, Bush, twenty years old, married Barbara Pierce, who was nineteen.

George Bush's rise to the presidency began in the oil fields of Texas where he went after graduating from Yale with hopes of making his own fortune in business. For nearly twenty years, Bush worked in the oil business, eventually building a million-dollar company and a reputation as a savvy businessman. In 1967 he made a successful run for a seat in the House of Representatives. Four years in the House were followed by appointment as ambassador to the United Nations and, later, as chief liaison to China. In 1976 Bush became director of the CIA, a position which he held for two years. In 1980, after his own unsuccessful run for the Republican presidential nomination, Bush accepted nomination as vice president and ran with Ronald Reagan against Jimmy Carter.

In 1988, after eight years under the shadow of Ronald Reagan, Bush emerged as a tough-minded, confident leader. President Bush shone in the world arena at a time when international issues dominated the news. In Panama, Bush launched a strong U.S. attack in retaliation to hostilities perpetrated by General Noriega on American military personnel. Bush also led the U.S. in a war to liberate Kuwait from the invading forces of Saddam Hussein's Iraq. The Gulf War was President Bush's greatest hour. Patriotic pride swept the nation, and the president's popularity soared. Bush also reaped the benefits of the end of the Cold War. As the Berlin Wall crumbled, the Soviet Union was dismantled, and countries across Eastern Europe installed democratic governments, Bush declared that a "new world order" was begun. Like Ronald Reagan before him, George Bush was regarded at home and abroad as a leader of great strength.

As the Gulf War receded from popular memory, however, and Americans began to focus on the economic troubles they faced at home, George Bush faced a difficult battle for reelection. In November of 1992, he lost that battle to Arkansas Democrat Bill Clinton.

We stand today at a unique and extraordinary moment. The crisis in the Persian Gulf, as grave as it is, also offers a rare opportunity to move toward an historic period of cooperation. Out of these troubled times . . . a new world order can emerge: a new era, freer from the threat of terror, stronger in the pursuit of justice, and more secure in the quest for peace. An era in which the nations of the world, east and west, north and south, can prosper and live in harmony. A hundred generations have searched for this elusive path to peace, while a thousand wars raged across the span of human endeavor. Today that new world is struggling to be born. A world quite different from the one we've known. A world where the rule of law supplants the rule of the jungle. A world in which nations recognize the shared responsibility for freedom and justice. A world where the strong respect the rights of the weak.

George Bush, speaking on the crisis in the Persian Gulf in 1990

George Bush and his wife Barbara raised five children, including George W., who went on to become the forty-third president of the United States, and Jeb, who went on to become governor of Florida. During their years in the White House, enjoyed frequent visits from their many grandchildren. Mrs. Bush was extremely popular with the American people, who embraced her for her no-nonsense style and her devotion to her family. Mrs. Bush did a great deal of work to promote adult literacy programs and also devoted her energies to Head Start and other children's education programs. George and Barbara Bush are pictured here at Bush's inaugural ceremony, seated alongside Vice President Dan Quayle and his wife, Marilyn.

Bill Clinton married his Yale Law School classmate Hillary Rodham in 1975 while both were professors of law at the University of Arkansas. Hillary Rodham Clinton, like her husband, was an ambitious overachiever. After law school she worked in Cambridge, Massachusetts, for the Children's Defense Fund and in Washington, D.C., for the House Judiciary Committee investigating President Nixon's role in Watergate. While her husband was governor of Arkansas, Mrs. Clinton became one of the most powerful attorneys in Arkansas. Once the Clinton family moved to the White House, she devoted most of her energies to the effort to reform the American health care system. Controversial for the powerful role she assumed in her husband's administration, Hillary Clinton wrote a new chapter in the history of the American first lady. Bill and Hillary Clinton have one daughter, Chelsea, born while her father was governor of Arkansas.

Our democracy must be not only the envy of the world but the engine of our own renewal. There is nothing wrong with America that cannot be cured by what is right with America. And so today we pledge an end to an era of deadlock and drift, and a new season of American renewal has begun.

To renew America we must be bold. We must do what no generation has had to do before. We must invest more in our own people—in their jobs and in their future—and at the same time cut our massive debt. And we must do so in a world in which we must compete for every opportunity. It will not be easy. It will require sacrifice. But it can be done and done fairly. Not choosing sacrifice for its own sake but for our own sake, we must provide for our nation the way a family provides for its children.

Our founders saw themselves in the light of posterity. We can do no less. Anyone who has ever watched a child's eyes wander into sleep knows what posterity is. Posterity is the world to come; the world for whom we hold our ideals, from whom we have borrowed our planet and to whom we bear a sacred responsibility. We must do what America does best: offer more opportunity to all and demand more responsibility from all.

from Bill Clinton's Inaugural Address,
delivered January 20, 1993

WILLIAM J. CLINTON

1946–
FORTY-SECOND PRESIDENT 1993–2001

Forty-second president William Jefferson Blythe Clinton was born in Hope, Arkansas, in 1946. He grew up in Hope and nearby Hot Springs with his mother, Virginia Blythe Clinton, and his stepfather, Roger Clinton. Clinton's natural father, William Jefferson Blythe, was killed in an automobile accident before his son was born. Inspired by the sixties leaders John F. Kennedy and Martin Luther King, Bill Clinton took an early interest in public service.

A bright and ambitious student, Clinton chose Georgetown University because of its location in Washington, D.C., and its respected programs in foreign service. At Georgetown, Clinton was a superior student. He was active in student government and served as an intern for Senator Fulbright of Arkansas. In 1968, shortly before his graduation, he performed volunteer relief work for the Red Cross during the riots that followed the assassination of Martin Luther King. After graduation, Clinton went to Oxford University in England as a Rhodes Scholar and traveled through much of Europe and the Soviet Union. Upon his return to America, he enrolled in Yale Law School, where three years later he earned his degree.

Bill Clinton began his career as a law professor at the University of Arkansas; but within four years he won his first elected office, that of the attorney general of Arkansas. Two years later, in 1978, at the age of thirty-two, Clinton won Arkansas's highest office and became the youngest governor in the United States. Governor Clinton was voted out of office after only one term, but in 1983 he again won the confidence of the people of Arkansas and returned to the governor's office, where he would remain for nine years.

Bill Clinton won the 1992 presidential election against George Bush in a campaign that focused on the nation's domestic troubles. Bush had achieved great popularity for his leadership in the Gulf War, but with the recession worsening across the country, Americans turned their thoughts to the economy and blamed Bush for its failures. Bill Clinton won a comfortable victory in a three-way race that included, along with President George Bush, Independent Texas businessman Ross Perot.

In his declaration of candidacy in 1991, Clinton stated "I refuse to be part of a generation that celebrates the death of communism abroad with the loss of the American Dream at home." In January of 1993 he assumed the presidency with an ambitious pledge to revive the economy, reduce the national debt, and create a national health care system that guarantees insurance to all Americans.

Bill Clinton served two terms as president. He presided over a period of continuous economic growth, an eight-year span during which the national budget went from a period of enormous deficit to the largest surplus in history and unemployment reached a forty-year low. He failed to institute the national health care system that he had promised during the campaign, but did have success with several related measures, including the Family and Medical Leave Act and the Children's Health Insurance Program.

The Clinton presidency will likely be remembered best, however, for the personal scandals which threatened the president's tenure. In 1999, Clinton became the second American president in history to face impeachment. Tried by the United States Senate on charges of perjury and obstruction of justice stemming from what Clinton himself called an "inappropriate relationship" with a White House intern, the president was acquitted in February of 1999.

GEORGE W. BUSH

1946–

FORTY-THIRD PRESIDENT 2001–2009

George W. Bush, the forty-third American president, entered the White House in January of 2001 familiar with the office of the presidency. From 1989 to 1993 his father, George Herbert Walker Bush, held the nation's highest office. The Bushes are only the second father-and-son pair in American history to serve as presidents.

Born in Connecticut but raised mostly in Texas, Bush followed his father's illustrious footsteps into Phillips Academy in Andover, Massachusetts, and Yale University in Connecticut. He then went on to earn an MBA at Harvard Business School before returning to Texas to begin a career in the oil business. In 1975, Bush founded an oil and gas exploration company and through the 1980s focused on building that company. In 1989, after a failed attempt at a seat in Congress, Bush became managing general partner of the Texas Rangers professional baseball team. Not until 1994 did he win his first elected office as governor of Texas. In 1998 he won a second term as governor but interrupted this term to seek the American presidency in 2000.

As governor of Texas, Bush characterized himself as a "compassionate conservative" and cited beliefs in limited government, personal responsibility, strong families, and local governmental control as his guiding principles. He worked to end lawsuit abuse, to strengthen public schools through the local communities, to reform welfare, and to strengthen the juvenile justice system.

These same concerns were the cornerstones of Bush's presidential campaign. Running against Democrat Vice President Albert Gore, Jr., of Tennessee, Bush promised new federal income tax cuts, a reduced federal bureaucracy, and higher literacy standards for public schools. He also pledged to revitalize the military and repair the Social Security system.

When voting polls closed on November 7, 2000, and the votes were tallied, Gore was the winner of the national popular vote by just over 300,000 ballots, but because of disputes in Florida, neither candidate had earned enough electoral votes to be declared victorious.

It would be thirty-six days before a winner emerged, and the contest in Florida moved from the voting booth to the courtroom. Legal teams representing both Bush and Gore brought arguments before Florida's state courts and supreme court. On December 13, 2000, the court reversed a Florida Supreme Court decision requiring a statewide manual recount of more than 170,000 undervotes—ballots for which the machine registered either no vote for president or a double vote. After this ruling, Vice President Gore conceded in the Florida contest, thus giving George W. Bush the necessary electoral votes to become the first American president of the twenty-first century.

Initially Bush's greatest challenge in office appeared to be repairing the party divisions created by the highly contested election. Soon those concerns were overshadowed by more serious events: the terrorist attacks at the World Trade Center and the Pentagon on September 11, 2001, and the resulting war on terror in Afghanistan and Iraq.

Married in 1977 to Laura Welch Bush, a teacher and librarian from Midland, Texas, Bush has looked to his wife as a close advisor. George W. and Laura Bush have twin daughters, Jenna and Barbara, who are named after their grandmothers.

George W. Bush is only the second President in United States history to also be the son of a former president. During the presidential campaign in 1988 and again in 1992, he served as an advisor to his father and helped lead his campaigns.

George Walker Bush and George Herbert Walker Bush are pictured at the Bush family home in Kennebunkport, Maine.

The Iraqi conflict became a flashpoint in the 2004 election campaign. In addition to his pledge to stay the course in the war on terror, Bush vowed to strengthen families by providing additional jobs, tax and Social Security reform, and increased access to healthcare. Bush's "Agenda for America" rang true with the American public, and on November 2, 2004, George W. Bush was elected to a second term.

As Bush's second term began, the economy was experiencing a period of growth and recovery after the decline that followed 9/11. Challenges were on the horizon, however, with an increase in subprime loans and a number of natural disasters. In August 2005, Hurricane Katrina hit the Gulf Coast, breaching New Orleans's levee system and resulting in more than 1,800 deaths and $80 billion in damages. Hurricanes Rita, Gustav, and Ike followed in the next three years, all hitting the Gulf Coast and interrupting the oil refineries and offshore drilling. As the war in Iraq wore on, a surge in U.S. troops into Iraq, begun in February 2007, brought a decrease in troop casualties and more safety and stability to the country. In 2008, as Bush headed into his final months in office, increasing defaults of subprime mortgages and decreasing home values brought the once vibrant housing market to the point of collapse. That, coupled with the ensuing credit crisis throughout the world, thrust the U.S. into an economic downturn that resulted in rising unemployment, loss of consumer confidence, fears of inflation, and some of the largest drops seen in the stock market since the Great Depression. As the U.S. grew weary of war and of economic and natural disasters, President Bush left office with one of the lowest approval ratings in modern history.

Today, our fellow citizens, our way of life, our very freedom came under attack in a series of deliberate and deadly terrorist acts. The victims were in airplanes, or in their offices; secretaries, businessmen and women, military and federal workers; moms and dads, friends and neighbors. Thousands of lives were suddenly ended by evil, despicable acts of terror.

The pictures of airplanes flying into buildings, fires burning, huge structures collapsing, have filled us with disbelief, terrible sadness, and a quiet, unyielding anger. These acts of mass murder were intended to frighten our nation into chaos and retreat. But they have failed; our country is strong.

A great people has been moved to defend a great nation. Terrorist attacks can shake the foundations of our biggest buildings, but they cannot touch the foundation of America. These acts shattered steel, but they cannot dent the steel of American resolve.

America was targeted for attack because we're the brightest beacon for freedom and opportunity in the world. And no one will keep that light from shining.

from President Bush's Address to the Nation
September 11, 2001

BARACK H. OBAMA

1961–

FORTY-FOURTH PRESIDENT 2009–

Barack Obama is the first African American elected to the presidency of the United States and came to the office by way of an international upbringing and an unconventional family history.

Barack Obama was born on August 4, 1961, in Honolulu, Hawaii, to Stanley Ann Dunham and Barack Obama Sr., both students at the University of Hawaii. Two years after his son's birth, the elder Obama returned to his native Kenya, and young Barack would see his father only once more, at the age of ten.

After his mother remarried, she and Barack moved to Jakarta, Indonesia, to live with his stepfather and younger half-sister. At the age of ten, Obama returned to Honolulu to live with his grandparents, and his mother and sister later joined him. He entered Occidental College in Los Angeles but transferred to Columbia University after two years. After graduation, Obama moved to Chicago where he became a community organizer on Chicago's South Side. In 1988 he entered Harvard Law School and was elected the first African American president of the *Harvard Law Review*. He received his J.D. in 1991, graduating magna cum laude.

Obama returned to Chicago, where he practiced law and taught at the University of Chicago. In 1996 he won a seat in the Illinois State Senate, serving for eight years. In 2004 he was elected to the U.S. Senate, becoming only the third African American since the Reconstruction to be elected to the Senate. Obama gave the keynote address at the 2004 Democratic convention, a speech that propelled him to national prominence and laid the groundwork for his presidential campaign and election in 2008.

By election night the country had sunk into a deep recession and many of Obama's early actions were directed toward moving the economy forward. Shortly after his inauguration, Obama used $79 billion of the $700 billion TARP funds (passed in the Bush administration) to rescue struggling automakers. Less than a month after taking office, Obama signed into law the American Recovery and Reinvestment Act, which set aside nearly $800 billion in an effort to stimulate the economy through tax cuts and funding for infrastructure projects and entitlement programs. And on July 21, 2010, Obama signed into law the Dodd-Frank Wall Street Reform and Consumer Protection Act, designed to prevent financial meltdowns such as that which occurred in September 2008. Although Obama began his term in a recession that was technically over June 2009, the recovery that followed was the weakest in U.S. history and throughout his first term the stubborn unemployment continued.

Obama's signature legislation, the Patient Protection and Affordable Care Act, was signed into law on March 23, 2010. The program, commonly known as "Obamacare," seeks to provide quality, affordable health care for all Americans while bringing down rising costs.

Ten months after his inauguration, Obama was awarded the Nobel Peace Prize for his "extraordinary efforts to strengthen international diplomacy and cooperation between peoples." Throughout his first term, he faced many challenges in the international arena. One of the country's ongoing threats was Iran's continued development of a nuclear weapon. As a candidate, Obama promised to pull troops out of Iraq and make Afghanistan a key focus of his foreign policy. The last U.S. troops pulled out of Iraq in December 2011, and troops are slated to pull out of Afghanistan by 2014.

In December 2010 the Middle East exploded in revolutions that would become known as the "Arab Spring." Violence took down the leaders of Egypt, Libya, Tunisia, and Yemen. The administration publicly supported the protests, but military support was limited to Libya. At the direction of President Obama, in May 2012, Osama bin Laden, the leader of al-Qaeda who had eluded the American military for nearly a decade, was shot and killed in Pakistan by American forces.

Barack Obama met his wife, Michelle, in 1989, when he was a summer associate at the Chicago law firm of Sidley Austin, where she worked. They were married in October 1992 and, until his inauguration, lived in Kenwood on Chicago's South Side with their daughters, Malia and Sasha.

On September 11, 2012, the eleventh anniversary of the 9/11 attacks, terrorists in several Middle Eastern countries stormed United States embassies. The worst attack was in Benghazi, Libya, where the U.S. ambassador and three other Americans were killed. In the aftermath of the attacks, questions arose as to the administration's response, and a controversy ensued throughout the last weeks of the presidential campaign.

Barack Obama was elected to a second term in office on November 6, 2012.

That we are in the midst of crisis is now well understood. Our nation is at war against a far-reaching network of violence and hatred. Our economy is badly weakened, a consequence of greed and irresponsibility on the part of some, but also our collective failure to make hard choices and prepare the nation for a new age.

Homes have been lost, jobs shed, businesses shuttered. Our health care is too costly, our schools fail too many—and each day brings further evidence that the ways we use energy strengthen our adversaries and threaten our planet.

. . . Less measurable, but no less profound, is a sapping of confidence across our land; a nagging

fear that America's decline is inevitable, that the next generation must lower its sights.

Today I say to you that the challenges we face are real. . . . The state of our economy calls for action, bold and swift. And we will act, not only to create new jobs, but to lay a new foundation for growth. . . .

Let it be said by our children's children that when we were tested we refused to let this journey end, that we did not turn back nor did we falter; and with eyes fixed on the horizon and God's grace upon us, we carried forth that great gift of freedom and delivered it safely to future generations.

from Barack Obama's first Inaugural Address, delivered January 20, 2009

List of Presidents, Vice Presidents, and First Ladies

GEORGE WASHINGTON | 1st President 1789–1797
Born February 22, 1732, Westmoreland County, Virginia
Died December 14, 1799, Mount Vernon, Virginia
Vice President: John Adams
First Lady: Martha Dandridge Custis Washington

JOHN ADAMS | 2nd President 1797–1801
Born October 30, 1735, Braintree (now Quincy), Massachusetts
Died July 4, 1826, Quincy, Massachusetts
Vice President: Thomas Jefferson
First Lady: Abigail Smith Adams

THOMAS JEFFERSON | 3rd President 1801–1809
Born April 13, 1743, Albemarle County, Virginia
Died July 4, 1826, Charlottesville, Virginia
Vice President: Aaron Burr (1801–1804); George Clinton (1804–1809)
First Lady: None
Wife: Martha Wayles Skelton Jefferson, Died 1782

JAMES MADISON | 4th President 1809–1817
Born March 16, 1751, Port Conway, Virginia
Died June 28, 1836, Montpelier, Virginia
Vice President: George Clinton (1809–1813); Elbridge Gerry (1813–1817)
First Lady: Dolley Payne Madison

JAMES MONROE | 5th President 1817–1825
Born April 28, 1758, Westmoreland County, Virginia
Died July 4, 1831, New York, New York
Vice President: Daniel D. Tompkins
First Lady: Elizabeth Kortright Monroe

JOHN QUINCY ADAMS | 6th President 1825–1829
Born July 11, 1767, Quincy, Massachusetts
Died February 23, 1848, Washington, D.C.
Vice President: John C. Calhoun
First Lady: Louisa Johnson Adams

ANDREW JACKSON | 7th President 1829–1837
Born March 15, 1767, The Waxhaws, South Carolina
Died June 8, 1845, Nashville, Tennessee
Vice President: John C. Calhoun (1829–1832);
Martin Van Buren (1832–1837)
First Lady: None
Wife: Rachel Donelson Robards, Died 1828

MARTIN VAN BUREN | 8th President 1837–1841
Born December 5, 1782, Kinderhook, New York
Died July 24, 1862, Kinderhook, New York
Vice President: Richard M. Johnson
First Lady: Angelica Van Buren (daughter-in-law)
Wife: Hannah Hoes Van Buren, Died 1819

WILLIAM HENRY HARRISON | 9th President 1841
Born February 9, 1773, Berkeley, Virginia
Died April 4, 1841, Washington, D.C.
Vice President: John Tyler (1841)
First Lady: Anna Tuthill Symmes Harrison

JOHN TYLER | 10th President 1841–1845
Born March 29, 1790, Charles City County, Virginia
Died January 18, 1862, Richmond, Virginia
Vice President: None
First Lady: Letitia Christian Tyler, Died 1842
First Lady: Julia Gardiner Tyler, Married 1844

JAMES K. POLK | 11th President 1845–1849
Born November 2, 1795, Mecklenburg County, North Carolina
Died June 15, 1849, Nashville, Tennessee
Vice President: George M. Dallas
First Lady: Sarah Childress Polk

ZACHARY TAYLOR | 12th President 1849–1850
Born November 24, 1784, Montebello, Virginia
Died July 9, 1850, Washington, D.C.
Vice President: Millard Fillmore (1849–1850)
First Lady: Margaret Mackall Smith Taylor

MILLARD FILLMORE | 13th President 1850–1853
Born January 7, 1800, Cayuga County, New York
Died March 8, 1874, Buffalo, New York
Vice President: None
First Lady: Abigail Powers Fillmore

FRANKLIN PIERCE | 14th President 1853–1857
Born November 23, 1804, Hillsborough, New Hampshire
Died October 8, 1869, Concord, New Hampshire
Vice President: William R. King (1853), Died April 18, 1853
First Lady: Jane Means Appleton Pierce

JAMES BUCHANAN | 15th President 1857–1861
Born April 23, 1791, Cove Gap, Pennsylvania
Died June 1, 1868, Lancaster, Pennsylvania
Vice President: John C. Breckinridge
First Lady: Harriet Lane (niece)

ABRAHAM LINCOLN | 16th President 1861–1865
Born February 12, 1809, Hardin County, Kentucky
Died April 15, 1865, Washington, D.C.
Vice President: Hannibal Hamlin (1861–1865); Andrew Johnson (1865)
First Lady: Mary Todd Lincoln

ANDREW JOHNSON | 17th President 1865–1869
Born December 29, 1808, Raleigh, North Carolina
Died July 31, 1875, Carter County, Tennessee
Vice President: None
First Lady: Eliza McCardle Johnson

ULYSSES S. GRANT | 18th President 1869–1877
Born April 27, 1822, Point Pleasant, Ohio
Died July 23, 1885, Mount McGregor, New York
Vice President: Schuyler Colfax (1869–1873);
Henry Wilson (1873–1875), Died 1875
First Lady: Julia Boggs Dent Grant

RUTHERFORD B. HAYES | 19th President 1877–1881
Born October 4, 1822, Delaware, Ohio
Died January 17, 1893, Fremont, Ohio
Vice President: William A. Wheeler
First Lady: Lucy Webb Hayes

JAMES A. GARFIELD | 20th President 1881
Born November 19, 1831, Orange Township, Ohio
Died September 19, 1881, Elberon, New Jersey
Vice President: Chester A. Arthur (1881)
First Lady: Lucretia Rudolph Garfield

CHESTER A. ARTHUR | 21st President 1881–1885
Born October 5, 1829, North Fairfield, Vermont
Died November 18, 1886, New York, New York
Vice President: None
First Lady: Ellen Lewis Herndon Arthur

GROVER CLEVELAND | 22nd President 1885–1889
Born March 18, 1837, Caldwell, New Jersey
Died June 24, 1908, Princeton, New Jersey
Vice President: Thomas A. Hendricks (1885)
First Lady: Frances Folsom Cleveland

BENJAMIN HARRISON | 23rd President 1889–1893
Born August 20, 1833, North Bend, Ohio
Died March 13, 1901, Indianapolis, Indiana
Vice President: Levi P. Morton
First Lady: Caroline Scott Harrison

GROVER CLEVELAND | 24th President 1893–1897
Born March 18, 1837, Caldwell, New Jersey
Died June 24, 1908, Princeton, New Jersey
Vice President: Adlai E. Stevenson
First Lady: Frances Folsom Cleveland

WILLIAM McKINLEY | 25th President 1897–1901
Born January 29, 1843, Niles, Ohio
Died September 14, 1901, Buffalo, New York
Vice President: Garret A. Hobart (1897–1901); Theodore Roosevelt (1901)
First Lady: Ida Saxton McKinley

THEODORE ROOSEVELT | 26th President 1901–1909
Born October 27, 1858, New York, New York
Died January 6, 1919, Oyster Bay, New York
Vice President: Charles W. Fairbanks (1905–1909)
First Lady: Edith Kermit Carow Roosevelt

WILLIAM H. TAFT | 27th President 1909–1913
Born September 15, 1857, Cincinnati, Ohio
Died March 8, 1930, Washington, D.C.
Vice President: James S. Sherman
First Lady: Helen "Nellie" Herron Taft

WOODROW WILSON | 28th President 1913–1921
Born December 28, 1856, Staunton, Virginia
Died February 3, 1924, Washington, D.C.
Vice President: Thomas R. Marshall
First Lady: Ellen Louise Axson Wilson, Died 1914
First Lady: Edith Bolling Galt Wilson, Married 1915

WARREN G. HARDING | 29th President 1921–1923
Born November 2, 1865, Bloomington Grove, Ohio
Died August 2, 1923, San Francisco, California
Vice President: Calvin Coolidge
First Lady: Florence Kling Harding

CALVIN COOLIDGE | 30th President 1923–1929
Born July 4, 1872, Plymouth Notch, Vermont
Died January 5, 1933, Northampton, Massachusetts
Vice President: Charles G. Dawes (1925–1929)
First Lady: Grace Goodue Coolidge

HERBERT HOOVER | 31st President 1929–1933
Born August 10, 1874, West Branch, Iowa
Died October 20, 1964, New York, New York
Vice President: Charles Curtis
First Lady: Lou Henry Hoover

FRANKLIN DELANO ROOSEVELT | 32nd President 1933–1945
Born January 30, 1882, Hyde Park, New York
Died April 12, 1945, Warm Springs, Georgia
Vice President: John Nance Garner (1933–1941); Henry Wallace (1941–1945); Harry S Truman (1945)
First Lady: Eleanor Roosevelt

HARRY S TRUMAN | 33rd President 1945–1953
Born May 8, 1884, Lamar, Missouri
Died December 26, 1972, Kansas City, Missouri
Vice President: Alben W. Barkley (1949–1953)
First Lady: Elizabeth "Bess" Virginia Wallace Truman

DWIGHT D. EISENHOWER | 34th President 1953–1961
Born October 14, 1890, Denison, Texas
Died March 28, 1969, Washington, D. C.
Vice President: Richard M. Nixon
First Lady: Marie "Mamie" Geneva Doud Eisenhower

JOHN F. KENNEDY | 35th President 1961–1963
Born May 29, 1917, Brookline, Massachusetts
Died November 22, 1963, Dallas, Texas
Vice President: Lyndon Baines Johnson
First Lady: Jacqueline Lee Bouvier Kennedy

LYNDON B. JOHNSON | 36th President 1963–1969
Born August 27, 1908, Johnson City, Texas
Died January 22, 1973, San Antonio, Texas
Vice President: Hubert Horatio Humphrey (1964–1969)
First Lady: Claudia Alta Taylor Johnson

RICHARD M. NIXON | 37th President 1969–1974
Born January 9, 1913, Yorba Linda, California
Died April 22, 1994, New York, New York
Vice President: Spiro T. Agnew (1968–1973); Gerald R. Ford (1973–1974)
First Lady: Thelma Catherine "Pat" Ryan Nixon

GERALD R. FORD | 38th President 1974–1977
Born July 14, 1913, Omaha, Nebraska
Died December 26, 2006, Rancho Mirage, California
Vice President: Nelson A. Rockefeller (1974–1977)
First Lady: Elizabeth Ann "Betty" Bloomer Ford

JIMMY CARTER | 39th President 1977–1981
Born October 1, 1924, Plains, Georgia
Vice President: Walter F. Mondale
First Lady: Eleanor Rosalynn Smith Carter

RONALD REAGAN | 40th President 1981–1989
Born February 6, 1911, Tampico, Illinois
Died June 5, 2004, Los Angeles, California
Vice President: George Herbert Walker Bush
First Lady: Nancy Davis Reagan

GEORGE H. W. BUSH | 41st President 1989–1993
Born June 12, 1924, Milton, Massachusetts
Vice President: J. Danforth Quayle
First Lady: Barbara Pierce Bush

WILLIAM J. CLINTON | 42nd President 1993–2001
Born August 19, 1946, Hope, Arkansas
Vice President: Albert Gore
First Lady: Hillary Rodham Clinton

GEORGE W. BUSH | 43rd President 2001–2009
Born July 6, 1946, New Haven, Conneticut
Vice President: Richard Cheney
First Lady: Laura Welch Bush

BARACK H. OBAMA | 44th President 2009–
Born August 4, 1961, Honolulu, Hawaii
Vice President: Joseph Biden
First Lady: Michelle LaVaughn Robinson Obama

INDEX

PHOTO CREDITS

4, Superstock; 5, Superstock; 6, Archive Photos; 7, Superstock; 8, Superstock; 9, The White House Historical Association/Portrait of Thomas Jefferson by Rembrandt Peale; 10, Archive Photos; 11, Superstock; 12, Superstock; 13, Archive Photos; 14, Archive Photos; 15, Superstock; 16, Archive Photos; 17, Archive Photos; 19, Archive Photos; 20, Superstock; 21, Archive Photos; 22, Archive Photos; 23, Superstock; 24, Superstock; 25, Archive Photos; 26, Superstock; 27, Superstock; 29, Superstock; 30, Archive Photos; 31, Superstock; 32, Archive Photos; 34, Superstock; 35, Archive Photos; 36, Superstock; 37, Superstock; 38, Superstock; 40, Archive Photos; 41, Superstock; 43, Archive Photos; 44, Superstock; 46, Archive Photos; 47, Superstock; 48, Superstock; 49, Superstock; 50, Archive Photos; 51, Archive Photos; 52, Archive Photos; 53, Superstock; 55, Archive Photos; 56, Archive Photos; 57, Superstock; 58, Archive Photos; 59, Archive Photos/American Stock Photo; 60, Archive Photos; 61, Superstock; 62, Superstock; 63, Archive Photos; 64, Superstock; 65, Superstock; 66, Archive Photos/Henri Dauman; 67, Superstock; 68, Archive Photos/Express Newspapers; 69, Superstock; 70, Archive Photos; 71, Superstock; 72, Archive Photos; 73, Superstock; 74, Official White House Portrait by Herbert E. Abrams; used by permission of White House Historical Association; 75, Superstock; 76, Archive Photos/American Stock Photo; 77, Archive Photos/Frank Edwards Fotos International; 78, Archive Photos; 79, Superstock; 80, Superstock; 81, Folio, Inc./Charlie Archambault; 82, Folio Inc./Jeffrey MacMillan; 83, Official White House photo by Eric Draper; 84, Official White House Photo by Pete Souza; 85, Scott Olson/Getty Images.